Sex,
Leadership
and Rock'n'Roll

Sex,
Leadership
and Rock'n'Roll

Leadership lessons from the Academy of Rock

Peter Cook

Crown House Publishing Limited
www.crownhouse.co.uk

First published by

Crown House Publishing Ltd
Crown Buildings, Bancyfelin, Carmarthen, Wales, SA33 5ND, UK
www.crownhouse.co.uk

and

Crown House Publishing Company LLC
4 Berkeley Street, 1st Floor, Norwalk, CT 06850, USA
www.CHPUS.com

First published 2006, Reprinted 2006

British Library of Cataloguing-in-Publication Data
A catalogue entry for this book is available
from the British Library.

10-digit ISBN 1845900162
13-digit ISBN 978-184590016-8

LCCN 2005931939

Printed and bound in Wales by
Gomer Press, Llandysul

For Alison, Thomas and James

The best dream I ever had

Keep on keepin' on!!

Acknowledgements

Many people have contributed unconsciously or deliberately to this work, and I would like to extend my special thanks to a few of them:

First and foremost to my wife Alison and my two children Thomas and James, without whose support, creativity, critique, playfulness, ruthless honesty and pragmatism there would be no end product. They are the inspiration for much of what I have been able to achieve and a constant reminder of the need for humanity, humility, soul and attitude at work.

I would also like to express my gratitude to Crown House Publishing, in particular Jill Owen, Caroline Lenton, Clare Jenkins, Rosalie Williams and Tom Fitton. Jill spotted the idea. Caroline and Clare had the foresight to see something in what I brought them, the doggedness to get it out of me in a form that could be published and the charm to keep the relationship going over an extended period. Rosalie championed the marketing and Tom brought the text to life using well-crafted graphics that do more than words ever can.

I was especially lucky to have a group of critical readers who were just that – they systematically tightened, loosened, provoked, advised and taunted the vital parts needed to write this book. They are: Claire Berry, Simon Clayton, Sue Constant, Andy Dolden, Peter McKenna, Matt Overton, Bridget Somers and Peter Young.

Special thanks also to the people who have contributed cases and materials to the book: IDEO Corporation, Argenta Ltd, Maverick Training and my friends Peter Birkett and Steve Crispe, who provided the photographs. These contributions bring the subject to life in a way that could not otherwise be achieved.

Finally, I would like to thank all those that I have been fortunate enough to work with in a wide range of businesses and rock bands. They have helped me to develop my knowledge, skills and wisdom in this area. All have contributed in their own way to this book.

Peter Cook

Contents

How do you take a group of 300 people on the most sexy Rock'n'Roll trip on the planet when you've got a quarter of a million pound hole in your budget? That is where this book comes in and thank goodness I've got it.

Foreword

In his book Peter has written some lovely flattering things about me and my ability to identify goals and achieve them. It would appear that I have been an inspiration to him. It is now his turn.

His book could not have been given to me at a more appropriate time. I have identified a goal and need what some might call a miracle to do the achieving bit. I have this dream of taking my own plane around the world and playing the greatest venues on the planet. Because I'm chartering my own jet, I can have 'OT-AIR' emblazoned on the tail, and, because I'm not particularly famous in certain parts of the globe, I have the luxury of taking my own audience with me!

Honestly, for a micro-star like myself, flying the world in my own jet is ridiculously sexy. I'm addicted to it and it is very, very Rock'n'Roll. These are precisely the themes that Peter has picked up in his book.

A lot of my fans agree that the tour is a sexy idea and have bought a planeload of John Otway World Tour tickets. I've done a deal for *Otway the Movie* based on the tour and have recorded the OT-AIR album to celebrate the trip of a lifetime.

Unfortunately, I did not take the weather and the effects of the recent wave of hurricanes into account. The huge hike in the cost of aviation fuel means that the cost of my jet has now risen by £200,000 from when we were first quoted on it. Like most people handling a project of this magnitude, I planned for some price rises, but not a near doubling of the costs.

So, the question is: how do you take a group of 300 people on the most sexy Rock'n'Roll trip on the planet when you've got a quarter-million pound hole in your budget? That is where this book comes in – and thank goodness I've got it! I'm now going to read it for some inspiration to help get this unique tour off the ground.

Does this book work? Well, if Peter and I take off next year, it obviously does!

October 2005

Preface

'Sex, Leadership and Rock'n'Roll – can life be that simple?'

'Not really. You need to know why you're doing what you do as well.'

'Does leadership benefit from an MBA?'

'Yes, but no. You need attitude and soul as well …'

'So the secret of leadership is not only technique but also attitude?'

'Er, definitely maybe …'

MBAs give you access to the special knowledge and rationale behind business, but they sometimes miss out on the attitude necessary to lead. By combining what business gurus say with the wisdom of the 3M Corporation, where our gurus are Madonna, Meat Loaf and Marley, we reach the point where the letters MBA stand for Management By Attitude. This rocks!

I want to take you on a journey in search of ideas that will alter your thinking. This book offers you a unique synthesis of leading-edge thinking plus earthy pragmatism to help you lead businesses where inspiration, perspiration and revolution are the norm. You will find this book especially valuable if you want to:

- increase levels and quality of creativity and innovation at work;
- access fresh thinking on old management chestnuts and cut through the jungle of buzzwords that beset the territory; and
- think differently about relationships, motivation, leadership and high-voltage performance.

This book has several moods and voices. In general, you will find more substantial material on the left-hand pages. To the right you will find summary materials that echo or are out of phase with the left side. You can therefore choose a fast route through the book or a more relaxed one, depending on your mood and preferences. I also use provocation, contradiction and the odd red herring to keep you on your toes. Don't therefore be surprised if our 3M model transforms into 4M, 6M and 7M before we reach the end. As the health warnings say: Caution! This product may contain nut(ty) remarks!

How did this begin? I gained my most valuable early learning directly from experience, through playing in rock bands and travelling the world to fix pharmaceutical factories. This meant dealing with senior people at a very early age. I had no training to help me do this and had to improvise to survive. In this respect, my training in rock bands was more important than anything I learned later in the MBA and other formal learning. I continue to dabble with music, performing in bands such as The Cowpokers – an unusual synthesis of country'n'western and glam-rock; a spoof heavy-metal band called Genital Sparrow; and with the punk icon John Otway. This is some kind of CPD (that's Can't Play the Drums yet, not Continuing Professional Development).

In the last twelve years, my company has developed the art and discipline of using music as a major or minor theme in our repertoire of approaches to strategic facilitation, learning, management development and conferences with a difference. In that time we've worked for organisations such as GSK, Pfizer, Kent County Council, Cookson Inc, The Metropolitan Police, Johnson and Johnson, The Royal College of Physicians, Allianz Cornhill, Electronic Arts and BP Amoco.

This book is necessarily the story so far, as this is an uncharted field. Good musicians and leaders never stop learning and I will be delighted to engage in a dialogue with those of you who learn best through conversation.

I can be contacted as follows:

telephone: + 44 (0)1634 855267 / 573788
email: mail@humandynamics.demon.co.uk
website: www.humandynamics.demon.co.uk

Peter Cook

August 2005

Prologue

Let it Rock!

The Concepts

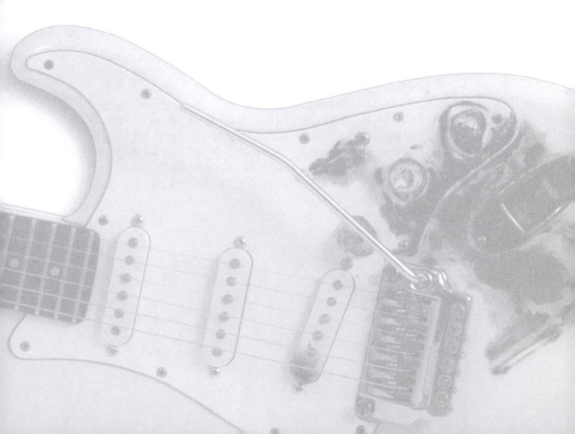

IBM burnt my guitar ...

Imagine IBM executives setting light to my Fender Stratocaster guitar at a leadership event.

Imagine a public services CEO who does Elvis impersonations for staff.

Imagine a pharmaceutical company chief who plays Rock'n'Roll.

Imagine a FTSE analyst who sings and plays the blues.

Are these fantasies? No ...

Joanne Moore is a financial analyst at FTSE. She is also an accomplished singer songwriter. Her ability to use the multiple intelligences that come from this diverse skillset is an undoubted asset when juggling the complexities and ambiguities associated with forecasting the future. This is especially so in a business environment such as the FTSE, which makes a huge impact on just about everything else. As for IBM, the CEO and the drug leader – well, that's what this book is about: the how, why, who, where, when and what next of Creative Leadership. Why, then, is music a relevant model for leaders?

Music is global language

Music has become global language in the last forty years. Moving across international and intercultural boundaries, it has replaced tribal ritual. Music brings communities together in ways that politicians and managers only dream of. There is simply no comparison between the energy and passion on the dance floor and that on the factory floor in many businesses. By contrast, the language of leadership put forward by so-called professional management consultants is dry, unnecessarily complex and does not rock. It's no surprise that it's neither understood nor embraced by the majority. It's time to cut the crap, start the rap and reach for something that engages both hearts and minds.

THE GLOBAL POWER OF MUSIC

JUST THINK ABOUT THE ENDURING POWER THAT BAND AID HAS HAD IN FOCUSING THE WHOLE WORLD ON FAMINE IN AFRICA

THE LOCAL POWER OF MUSIC

'Scuse me while I kiss the sky

THE AUTHOR'S FENDER STRATOCASTER AFTER ITS CREMATION BY IBM LEADERS

Music reflects the culture of the age

Music comes from the street. It mirrors popular culture and matches the pace of change in modern society and the ways in which businesses must respond if they are to survive. We experience shorter and shorter product lifecycles and must be prepared to engage with this fact if we are to stay ahead of the innovation game. In such a world:

- Leaders must be able to move elegantly from the conceptual clouds to the pragmatic gutter and back again. Keeping your feet on the ground is not an excuse for micromanagement.

- Strategy must synthesise long-term vision with short-term expediency. This is not the same as being led by management fads and fashions.

Music touches the soul of business

We cannot directly see the impact of climate, culture and leadership style on the balance sheet. However, we can detect the impact of a business that is in tune with itself and its customers on a properly balanced scorecard, where learning is valued just as much as profit. The best corporate players have stopped sleepwalking into the future and are waking up to the fact that a focus on financials is not the only driver of corporate success. We increasingly see evidence that this actually damages long-term competitive advantage. Just look at Unilever's failed five-year improvement plan, which they called the 'Path to Growth'. It would be more aptly titled after Chris Rea's 'The Road to Hell'. I have been most impressed with their recent attempts to restore soul to their business. Are they now on a Stairway to Heaven?

Music is the language of our emotions. Leaders are responsible for aligning staff emotions with business ambitions – put crudely, for bringing the heart into contact with the head. While many businesses have lost their soul, the smart players recognise that the emotional alignment of their staff is the source of their future competitive strength. As The Beatles and James Brown might have said, 'Come together and funk'.

How does your business respond to all of this? Let's look at the Rock'n'Roll of business.

SOUL SACRIFICE

MUSIC IS THE LANGUAGE
OF OUR EMOTIONS. WE
ARE IN DANGER OF LOSING
THE ABILITY TO SPEAK THIS
LANGUAGE AS BUSINESSES
BECOME MORE CORPORATE.
SOME BUSINESSES HAVE
ALREADY LOST THEIR SOUL.

PETER COOK,
ACADEMY OF ROCK

5

The Rock'n'Roll of business ...

If Dylan were a business guru, he would have said, 'The times, they are a'changed'. If Prince were a management consultant, he would have pointed us at some of the major 'Signs o' the Times':

- Product and service life cycles are drastically shorter. In short, today's peacocks are tomorrow's feather dusters. Just think of Sony, considered one of the world's most innovative companies up to the end of the 20th century, currently in deep trouble. At the time of writing, Hewlett Packard, once untouchable, are also having to undergo major transformations.

- Markets are more fluid and global. Stuff moves round the globe at the speed of sound. Cheap is no longer always crap. Electrolux have had to move a good deal of their manufacturing out of Western Europe just to stay alive.

- Staff express themselves and ask, 'What can you do for me?' rather than only you asking them this question. Fail to answer them well and they leave.

- Consumers are more individual and promiscuous in their wants, whims, wishes, needs and fantasies. 'Loose' consumers switch partners.

Leading in such a business environment is no longer like conducting an orchestra, where the band has the same sheet music, players know what instruments they must play and the audience accept what they are given. In 21st century society, leaders must move from being score writers to becoming improvisers. Leading a rock band is the analogy of choice for this shift, since it suggests leaders should:

- improvise even when the overall strategy, constraints and outcomes are unclear, rather than doing nothing or choosing to retreat;

- leverage diverse and precocious talents from people who refuse to be managed but must work together if all are to prosper;

- create capacity for self-organisation, and for coherent and rapid change, so that people can develop innovations that fit the strategy, without constant nannying from the corporate nerve centre;

- tune into the world around them, picking up feedback from a variety of sources and daring to change course along the way; and

- have more productive fun at work, i.e. 'aha' (inspiring), 'ha, ha' (laughing), and 'cha, cha' (moving) moments. Get rockin'!

Wisdom from the Academy of Rock

Music is social history

Leadership is about changing social futures

The Rock'n'Roll approach brings popular culture and leadership together in ways that other approaches cannot reach.

Or, in the words of Academy of Rock Leadership Guru James Brown:

'Anyproblem in the world can be solved by dancing'

What do I get?

I'm simply offering you a compelling and more memorable way of learning about leadership and personal development so that you can:

- increase levels and quality of creativity at work;
- develop a culture where innovation is business as usual;
- access fresh thinking on old management chestnuts;
- cut through the jungle of buzzwords that mean anything and nothing;
- think differently about relationships at work, be they 1:1 or multichannel;
- get to grips with motivation and leadership;
- move staff beyond compliance to commitment and high-voltage performance; and
- consider how you can really get your business to learn, start over and reinvent itself.

In doing so, we'll bring together leading thinking from the business gurus with the earthy pragmatism of rock music. At the Academy of Rock our gurus come from the 4M Corporation, e.g. Madonna, Meat Loaf, Mozart and Marley. That's already one more M than the last time we mentioned the Academy of Rock! This will be a different ride through the business world. Enjoy!

We'll begin with a prelude on Creative Leadership. We'll dig into this topic more when we get hooked on Motivation and Leadership in the chapter called 'Dialogue 2: Drugs'.

The Academy of Rock approach

Business Gurus

+

the Power of Rock

=

Intelligent pragmatism

Earthy wisdom

New ways to see old stuff

Creative Leadership unplugged

■ *Creativity* at work means thinking novel and appropriate ideas, not just crazy ideas. This is the difference between a rock group that engages its audience and is successful, and one that plays solely for itself (usually in a bedroom) and isn't. In business, this means engaging profitably with clients' *wants*, while spending time discovering their known and unknown *needs*, so that you can maintain their interest over time. Take a walk on the wild side …

■ *Innovation* is the successful implementation of those ideas. This is the difference between a band that just plays in clubs and one that brings its music to the marketplace in ways that last beyond a one-hit wonder. In business, this means developing and delivering products and services that move beyond fad value. For example, although Atkins Nutritionals were seen as a major challenge to conventional slimming products with their Atkins Diet products, this did not prevent them from going into bankruptcy in 2005. There are three forms of innovation: *strategic innovation* – transforming the basis of competition, the brand or enterprise; *product or service innovation* – the exploitation of ideas to deliver something the marketplace wants or needs; and *process innovation* – new ways to do old things. What's new, pussycat?

■ *Creative Leadership* is about finding innovative strategies to address problems, opportunities, issues, challenges and concerns both inside and outside the enterprise. A successful band manages individual temperament differences, finds ways to make itself stand out from the crowd, responds to its audience etc. A successful business actively manages to address the ever-changing moods of the Three Cs: Customers, Clients and Colleagues. As Frank Sinatra might have sung, 'I did it their way.'

■ *Creative Leadership* is about the generation of a climate where people feel confident about thinking the unthinkable and making positive change. A rock group works mostly on emotional intelligence – feelings, listening, awareness of self and others. Leading businesses are aware of the all-pervading influence of climate. Creative leaders take positive steps to maintain such a climate. Is there something in the air?

Creative Leadership unplugged

Creativity

=

thinking differently

Innovation

=

converting that thinking into purposeful action

Leading Change

=

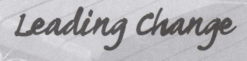

taking other people with you

Creative Leadership unplugged

Techniques for Creative Leadership have their place for boosting the climate for innovation and improving the level and quality of ideas in the enterprise. Yet we are talking mostly about attitude here rather than a bundle of MBA techniques, applied in a wooden way, without flair. In the same way, teaching people musical scales can be used to enhance dexterity, but no amount of technique will help overcome poor stage presence. Teaching people scales is different from learning to rock. It ain't what you do. It's the way that you do it?

High performance springs from difference = diversity. If we are to successfully innovate, we are talking teams of diverse people. Rock groups are composed of very different personalities; extraverts, introverts, structure freaks, improvisers etc. Successful businesses recognise the importance of differences. They encourage mixing between different professions and are prepared to handle, tolerate or encourage the Three Cs of diversity – the Confusions, Contradictions and Conflicts that this produces. 'Knowing me, knowing you?'

Using creativity to *solve problems* or *seek opportunities* requires us to detach ourselves and understand the real problem or opportunity before leaping in with the solution. In practice, staying detached can be one of the hardest things to do, since most of us are very much engaged or in the zone with the things that we hold dear. Detachment happens naturally in a musical performance, since good jamming requires the players to hear the Gestalt (big picture) within which they are able to make a relevant contribution. They are both 'in the zone' and 'out of it'. Most people at work are either permanently switched on or fully detached. It's rare to find people who can be both. When people realise the importance of the ability to become detached, and are given the space at work to use it, they will find opportunities for contemplating new business ideas or for reworking ineffective approaches. As the Byrds observed, eight miles high?

Creative Leadership unplugged

'21st century leadership is about creating compelling futures that mobilise people to take intelligent action'

Peter Cook

Rock'n'Roll businesses

Contrary to what some people think, musical improvisation is both structured and experimental. For example, twelve-bar blues has such a well-known basic structure that it's possible for musicians who have never rehearsed together to play as if they had known each other for years. This is not confined to the world of blues, rock or jazz – there are many parallels with experimental flamenco, Sufi improvisations, raga, hip-hop and salsa music.

Streetwise executives understand the links between improvisation and innovation. Word up:

> *… improvising with the band long into the night, I learned once again about the joys of stealing good ideas, of jumping all over some entirely serendipitous passage, hearing intriguing possibilities in someone's mistake …*

> *Jerry Hirshberg, President, Nissan Design International*

Hirshberg has made a very successful career in transferring this learning into the hard world of car design. He was responsible for producing a culture that fostered innovation, enabling his team to produce cutting-edge designs such as Nissan's Altima, Pathfinder, Quest and Maxima, Ford's Villager and Infiniti's J30. Hirshberg's comments illustrate the quality of structured looseness that is a key feature of successful improvisation.

Sears, Lockheed Martin, and Bristol Myers Squibb, have experimented with music to bring leadership and teamwork alive for top managers. Kodak, Arthur Andersen and Boeing used a poet to purge their inner leadership demons. Poetry offers another way of looking at familiar issues. Yet the power of music is that it brings together the lyrics of management with the music of leadership. In other words, it's a whole-brained rather than half-witted approach.

Music and genius

'If I were not a physicist,
I would probably be a musician.
I often think in music. I live
my daydreams in music.
I see my life in terms of music …
I get most joy in life out of music.'

Albert Einstein

Elected?

Here are some other signs that indicate that leaders understand the power of rock:

- The Japanese prime minister, Junichiro Koizumi, is an acknowledged heavy-metal fan and has been regarded as an agent of change for the country's ailing fortunes. He is unusual in his willingness to speak without a script in a country that normally expects greater formality from public figures. Ozzy Osbourne for UK prime minister? Prince for US president? Andrea Bocelli for Italian premier? Kraftwerk for German chancellors?

- Paul Simons, chairman and CEO of Ogilvy and Mather, a global brand in advertising, started life playing in rock bands. After hanging up his guitar at the age of twenty, he moved through a series of entrepreneurial roles. He observed that doing an MBA (Much Bigger Amps) and brand management was 'Rock'n'Roll of a different kind'. One of the things he learned playing in bands was the power of mass communication.

Others tried to rock but didn't let their hair down far enough:

- The Department of Trade and Industry (DTI) in the UK hired the Eurythmics to give a seminar on creativity and leadership. At a seminar entitled 'Fast Forward', civil servants were encouraged to unlock their creative potential to come up with new ideas to address old problems. Dave Stewart and Annie Lennox's brief intervention was insufficient to give the DTI the ability to free itself from red tape, inefficiency and a liking for more of the same. Perhaps Peter Gabriel's 'Sledgehammer' was needed! See page 177 for the wisdom of sledgehammers.

- The British Broadcasting Corporation (BBC) organised a series of 'Let's Rock It' events to focus the corporation on entrepreneurship and change. Better – but a couple of seminars were insufficient to change a corporation under constant vigilance from the public and increasingly from governments. Good try – but some heavy metal was required.

Let's look next at the similarities and differences between rock and other established music paradigms.

Heavy Metal Leaders

Junichiro Koizumi,
Japanese prime minister

Paul Simons, chairman and chief
executive of Ogilvy and Mather

Metallica, Motörhead
and Mud

The Department of Trade and
Industry?!

The BBC?

Mixing music and leadership

Although I'll focus on rock music, especially where improvisation is involved, I am also covering the wider spectrum. Other respectable souls have rightly noticed the connections between other forms of music and leadership. Let's bring them on …

In the beginning there were orchestras …

For the last two hundred years people have led enterprises as though they were orchestras. Obsessed by the need for order and control in the way work should be organised, they created structures into which people were fitted. Paint it Black or Simply Red, as Henry Ford would have said (but not Mellow Yellow or a Whiter Shade of Pale …). This meant that one person (the conductor) held the composer's operating instructions (the score). The performer's main role was to follow the score accurately and without deviation (improvisation). This analogy has remained attractive throughout the Industrial Revolution for the following reasons:

■ It gave **leaders** a feeling of absolute control and certainty about the future. This enabled leaders to make plans about long-term futures based on extrapolating from the past. Essentially, a top-down planning approach to corporate strategy.

■ It gave **followers** certainty about their role and required performance levels. Fixed job descriptions and performance management methods provide a rhythm and routine to daily life that let people know that they are doing what is required of them. Over time, such systems become unconscious structures or scores that create conformity and level performance to acceptable rather than extraordinary levels.

■ It gave **shareholders** a sense of direction and trust in the business strategy. Relatively few people want to buy shares in a company whose CEO stands up at the AGM and adapts a line from the Sweet classic 'Blockbuster', by saying, 'Hell, does anyone know the way? There's got to be a way … to increase top- and bottom-line performance.'

The orchestra analogy is essentially about conformity in terms of getting it right and collaboration around a set of instructions, in other words doing what you are told. Group identity is more important than individual stardom in an orchestra. The main questions an orchestra must ask itself are: 'Did we get it right?' and 'Did we give a good rendition of the composer's idea?'

ORCHESTRAS ARE MOSTLY ABOUT STRUCTURE

We **live** *in a* less **STRUCTURED** BUSINESS *world*

We need new models for getting things done in this environment.

It's the end of the world as we currently know it ...

How we respond will determine our success.

The orchestra analogy is useful when: the business environment and product/service mix are simple and stable; staff expectations of work and its meaning are low; minimum performance levels are required for economic success. But you may wonder how many enterprises fit this profile in the 21st century.

The orchestra analogy assumes that the conductor (the CEO) has the correct sheet music and is supremely good at conducting, and that the orchestra members are very good at following a preplanned score. However, that analogy is increasingly out of step with the way that innovative businesses get things done, because:

■ The CEO usually does not and cannot know everything required for establishing a top-down strategy. At best they have only *some* of the sheet music, or, even worse, may be using an outdated score. They may also be better at playing than conducting. This is the case in some businesses where leaders have previously been good practitioners.

■ These days you find staff who won't follow the conductor's directions. This is more likely if your current staff come from the so-called Generations X (people born between 1964 and 1981) and Y (post-1981). These people are noticeably different from the Baby Boomers (pre-1964). They crave change, challenge, hedonism, speed, instant gratification, progression and freedom. They are individualistic and reject traditional forms of leadership based on the command-and-control model. In short, they will not be pushed around, even if their bosses think it's good for them. Moreover, they are very aware of their market value and will walk if they think that they are not well catered for.

Although the orchestral analogy has some great parallels with rock music in terms of structure and discipline, it also has some limitations in the modern context of complexity, chaos and what we expect of our leaders. So what else is out there? Let there be jazz …

Stravinsky Rocks!

'I have learned throughout my life as a composer chiefly through my mistakes and pursuits of false assumptions, not by my exposure to founts of wisdom and knowledge.' *Igor Stravinsky*

... and then there was jazz

John Kao noted the connections between jazz and leadership in his book *Jamming: The Art and Discipline of Business Creativity*. Kao is a Harvard Business School professor and jazz musician, and has a PhD in psychiatry from Yale University and a successful career in Hollywood. He points out that creativity is fuelled by contradictions: between discipline and freedom; convention and experiment; old and new; familiar and strange; expert and naïve; power and desire. He points out that leaders should not try to resolve contradictions but work with them.

Kao's vision is mostly about genius-level creativity – he uses Charlie Parker among his examples of successful freeform jazz musicians who operate at the edge of chaos. You have to be a brilliant player to be able to do this, and this points to one difficulty with the jazz analogy: that much business creativity is quite ordinary and does not always require or value genius-level contributions. Have you ever tried to get a bunch of experts to work together? Jazz can also be an elitist form of music and has many unwritten rules, whereas rock is less concerned with etiquette.

Both the orchestra and the jazz analogies offer us complementary insights into leadership. The Rock'n'Roll analogy is both structured and improvised, is more accessible as a popular art form and relates better to the less certain post-industrial society that we play in. The musical analogies of leadership range from the highly formal and structured through to informal and more chaotic. Rock'n'Roll sits in the middle, which is where most businesses are, both tight and loose ...

The Music–Business mix

Music analogy	Orchestral	Rock'n'Roll	Freeform Jazz
Aspects of the business analogy	• Stable bureaucracies • Scores • Group matters • More central leadership	• 21st century business • Scores and improvisation • Group and individual matter • Distributed leaders	• Organic structures • Edge of chaos • Individuals matter • Self organising leadership

Leadership and the Irish Jig

Irish composer and academic, Professor Ó'Súilleabháin, has also observed the contrast between the classical orchestra with the informality of traditional Irish music.

Irish music depends a good deal upon individuality and improvisation, although these take place within a system. Inside the system's rules, musicians are free to play, elaborate and diverge. Different players take the lead at different times. Players respond to each other dynamically, swapping lead and background roles. What looks anarchic and directionless has an underlying structure and form and can lead to something sublime.

In this sense, the Irish jig is part of our Rock'n'Roll analogy.

... so where does the Rock'n'Roll analogy score well?

The Rock'n'Roll analogy is essentially about breaking away from the score and doing your own thing within the context of the overall structure. Unlike the orchestra, the individual is as important as the group, although there are some star soloists.

The main questions a successful rock band must ask itself are: 'Did we stand out from the crowd?' and 'How was the performance?'

The Rock'n'Roll analogy is looser than the orchestra analogy, but not so chaotic that it needs the genius-level contributors required in the jazz analogy. It therefore offers maximum reach into the general population – just think how many of your staff will have been brought up on MTV. It also offers a number of advantages in the following areas:

■ Rock'n'Roll acknowledges the realities of work, e.g. the Three Cs of work: Competition, Contradiction and Conflagration, rather than the tidy but ineffective 'One Vision, One Mission' view of life. Conflict is good for performance just so long as it does not become an obsession or a purely personal battle.

■ Good rock music reflects its social period. It offers insights into the human dynamics of leadership without requiring you to undertake an MBA. If you have already done one, as I have, it offers the antidote to pure technique, so that you will be listened to at work. The combination of MBA + AOR (Academy of Rock) is especially powerful.

■ Rock is much more about engaging with and responding to consumer and customer needs. Jazz is typically more inwardly focused and orchestral music appropriately detached. Many university-led start-up companies in the new millennium saw themselves as freeform jazz entrepreneurs wanting to create musical fusion, only then to find that what they were offering was too advanced for most of the players and the audience.

I use 'Rock'n'Roll' in its widest sense in this book: I am not talking only about a particular genre of music here, but any form of music that uses improvisation as well as structure. In this sense, Rock'n'Roll includes soul, blues, salsa, funk, hip hop, drum'n'bass, gamelan orchestras and so on. From Mozart to Madonna; from Springsteen to Avril Lavigne; from Abba to AC/DC; from The Beach Boys to the Spice Girls; from Django to DJ Sammy; from BB King to Be-Bop Deluxe; from Hawkwind to Hendrix, from The Beatles to Beethoven; from Stravinsky to the Sex Pistols; from Tina Turner to Bachman Turner Overdrive to Bach; from Eno to ELO and Eminem; from Orbison to the Orb; from Holly to Frankie Goes to Hollywood; and so on.

Who's playing the drums and bass in your business while all your stars are busy playing solos and smashing up their guitars?

In other words …

Who is sustaining innovation while your key players are crashing into new markets and crucifying your budget?

From the Academy of Rock...

Tuning into innovation

Musically speaking: Score + Improvisation = Performance:

S + I = P

In music, structure is provided by the score and other predetermined elements such as tempo and dynamics. Improvisation comes out of the freedom to interpret and the ability to respond to the moment. Too much structure produces a dull rigid performance. Just think how many military marches get into the charts! Too much improvisation and the performance is too self-indulgent. This goes some way to explain why freeform jazz is a specialist interest.

If we translate this into the world of Creative Leadership, we get: Structure + Creativity = Innovation:

S + C = I

There is no implied order in this formula: sometimes innovation arises from a structured improvement of an existing product or service, and very little creativity is involved. In other cases, a flash of inspiration plus a lot of creative persistence is required to develop an innovative product or service. Breakthrough creativity is not obvious and often requires leadership to ensure the idea is not defeated along the way.

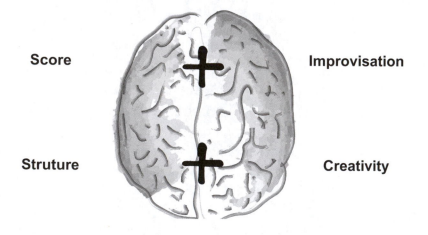

Score   **Improvisation**

Struture   **Creativity**

The formula uses both sides of our brain: the left, more logical, ordered, structured, Mr Spock side, and the right, more emotionally intelligent, intuitive, creative, improvised, Captain Kirk side.

Anarchy in the Academy of Rock

In music:

$$S + I = P$$

Score + Improvisation = Performance

In business:

$$S + C = I$$

Structure + Creativity = Innovation

Retuning into innovation

When we first looked at the S + I = P formula in music, we managed to ignore the audience. Oddly enough, this also happens in real life in bands who play music purely for themselves! However, star performers know that their audience is at least as important as their music. Of course, the same is true in business. So we will now re-examine the formula to reveal some further insights:

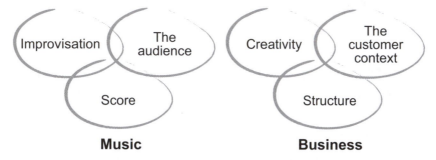

Music   **Business**

In music, there is an audience. In business, we have customers and a context for doing business. In a business that is in tune with itself, there will be a balance between creativity and structure to get things to the market and an overlap between what the audience/customer wants/needs, set in the context for doing successful business. These aspects are symbolised by balance and overlap in the model above. Let's now consider what happens when these elements are out of harmony with one another:

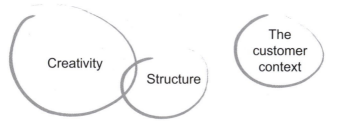

Too much creativity without structure and nothing ever gets finished!

Here we have the basic reason for so many first-wave dotcom failures, i.e. a business full of creatives but no structured people able to channel that creativity towards a market need. It's not smart to have a warehouse full of things that nobody wants or needs. Unfettered creativity accounts for a lot of product failures in this era. For example, just think about those so-called Innovations catalogues we are sent with products such as the 'Combined Tea Maker and Toenail Clipper' and the 'Self-Cleaning Integrated Moth Collector and DVD Player' – all things that I bet you want to own now that I've mentioned them!

Inventions the world did not ask for
(but may get now that they have been invented here)

Tropical iPod
(includes Lion
Taming Kit and
Snake Charmer
MPEG file)

The Self-Cleaning
Integrated Moth
Collector and
DVD Player

The
Self-Filling
Dustbin
and
Mail
Collector

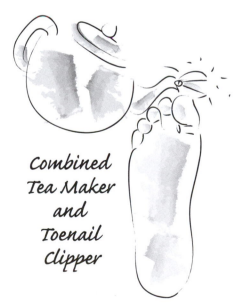

Combined
Tea Maker
and
Toenail
Clipper

The Instant
'Convert Your
U2 Songs to
Britney Spears
Dance Floor Music'

Now let's consider the opposite scenario:

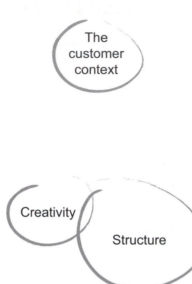

Too much structure without creativity and nothing ever gets started!

Here we have a model of how some public authorities still operate in the face of compelling pressure for greater responsiveness. Requests for improved services get pushed through the same committees, which silence the customer need and strangle new ideas before they have even had a chance to take root in the organisation. Of course, there are notable exceptions, and we will look at some of these later.

Have you got the balance between structure, creativity and customer context right at work?

If not, where does the balance need to be made better?

How might this be started?

Not only creativity but also structure

In music, too much structure produces a dull, rigid performance.

Too much improvisation and the band never get to play.

if they do,
physical violence from the
audience is usually involved
at some level as well ...

Summary

The traditional command-and-control model of leadership is broken. Creativity, Innovation, Leadership and Change are the driving forces of 21st century business.

21st century leadership is about adopting styles that balance people's needs for structure and ambiguity at work. To achieve this, leaders must move from being score writers to being improvisers. This requires a shift from the structured formality of the orchestra to the improvised structure of rock music. The two models can be generally contrasted as follows:

Orchestra analogy	Rock'n'Roll analogy
Performing your role accurately within the context of the structure	Doing your own thing within the context of the structure
The orchestra is more important than individual players – there are some star soloists	The individual is *as* important as the band – there are some star soloists
Group performance is paramount	Individual *and* group performance is paramount
Mostly centralised leadership in the form of a conductor, with a hierarchical structure of team leaders, for example, leader of wind section	Distributed leadership, which changes from time to time

Innovation requires both structure and creativity. Musicians who improvise operate within a set of explicit or unconscious rules, e.g. the rhythm, musical genre or some other foundation from which experimentation is safe. Leaders must ensure sufficient psychological safety if they are to unleash the Three Cs of Creativity, Commitment and Can-do.

Leaders must raise the skill level of the players and the level of the ensemble playing while paying attention to the audience response, even though what they say may not be to their liking.

the-importance-of-variation

John Bonham, drummer with Led Zeppelin, always
played slightly behind the beat. This is considered
to be one of the key features that gave their music
a much greater dynamic. Modern rhythm machines
allow programmers to simulate this sloppy timing. To
understand this point more clearly, listen to the track
'When The Levee Breaks' on the album *Led Zeppelin IV.*

Academy of Rock Guru Frank Zappa also
commented on creativity and variation:

'Without deviation, progress is not possible.'

He also said 'Hot Rats' but we have not yet worked
out the transferability of this piece of wisdom to
business improvement. Answers by email please.

Questions to ask back at the ranch

Three sets of questions to pose next time you're on stage:

1. What can you do about people who want to see the whole score before they are willing to invest their energy in a project or commit themselves to change? In other words, how do you provide sufficient structure for staff with a low tolerance for change?

2. What can you do about staff whose degree of improvisation around the score is so wildly expensive that it puts the business at risk? In other words, is it possible to be too creative at work? How can you stop your creatives wasting too many resources without switching them off for good?

3. How do you involve the audience – in other words, your customers and the market – in defining new and unknown product/service needs? How do you set up a dialogue for profitable partnerships?

Dialogue

Rock on ...

The Practice

In the beginning there was sex, then there was Rock'n'Roll, followed by leadership …

Well, I guess that some will say this is an oversimplification and the events were not exactly in this order. Nevertheless, my contention is that some business gurus have become increasingly indigestible and we need some fresh thinking on personal development and leadership. We don't need another spreadsheet, as Tina Turner might have put it. In this part of the book I've set out three simple but compelling analogies that provide a different set of lessons for leaders. Rather than the Master of Business Administration (MBA) this is Management By Attitude (MBA). The three analogies that make or break a business are these.

- **'Sex'** is about making, keeping and ending work relationships, drawing on leading-edge psychology that is easily digestible. We're talking romance, love and friendship under the 'sex' analogy rather than just whips, chains and hardcore, so it's OK to read on …

- **'Drugs'** is about motivating and leading others. 'Drugging yourself' is about reaching peak personal performance and 'drugging others' about engaging people in a shared ambition, i.e. leadership. Again, we're talking adrenaline and endorphins rather than smack, crack and cocaine here …

- **'Rock'n'Roll'** is about reaching and sustaining high performance. This includes delivery and execution skills, learning, unlearning and reinvention. No need to throw a TV out of your office window to get in the zone, however enjoyable that might be …

In other words:

LET'S TALK ABOUT SEX because LOVE IS THE DRUG so ROLL OVER, BEETHOVEN

So let's get on up …

Fed up with indigestible business gurus?

Want a fresh take on relationships?

Read everything on motivation and leadership?

Need to create a high-performance workplace?

The Academy of Rock exam paper

1) The phrase MBA stands for:

Master of Business Administration? ☒
More Bloody Analysis? ☒
Management By Attitude? ☑
Much Bigger Amps? ☑

(A+)

Musically speaking, an MBA
'don't mean a thing if it ain't
got that swing.'

Make sure your MBAs have attitude
as well as technique.

Dialogue 1

Sex

Rock on ...
Relationships

In the words of Salt and Pepa, 'Let's talk about sex.' However, I'm not suggesting you encourage office affairs to increase your bottom line. I simply use sex as a provocative analogy for looking at relationships, be they one-to-one or one-to-many. We're talking romance, love and friendship under the 'sex' headline rather than just uniforms and positions. In the words of the Sex Pistols, Marvin Gaye and T Rex 'Never mind the bollocks, Let's get it on.'

Let's talk about sex?

Rock'n'Roll is about scoring. To be brutally honest, the same is true at work. I don't mean laying office boys and girls. I *do* mean enchanting people in an honest exchange for a job, your products or services. We've left the age where all this was done naturally. Staff have attitude these days and ask, 'What can you do for me?' on Day One. It's a damned good question. Even better, if you can answer it properly and change the answer over time in tune with changing wants, needs and fantasies, they will commit to you and perform in ways that other businesses only dream of. What does this mean? How will rock give us better answers than the business gurus playing with themselves? My contention is that the sex analogy accurately describes what should be happening at work. In essence the same basic instincts apply:

1. **Foreplay**: Getting your Three Cs (Customers, Clients and Colleagues) engaged and excited with what you have to offer. Aligning expectations. Light my fire?

2. **Intercourse**: Working together, really communicating persuasively. Getting down and dirty. Delivering promises. Fire!

3. **Climax**: Achieving peak performance over and over. Again. And again. Relight my fire?

4. **Afterglow**: Clarifying gains, consolidating achievements, finding out how it was for them and adjusting accordingly. This virtuous circle moves the Three Cs (Customers, Clients and Colleagues) from one-night stands to long-term lovers. Fire brigade!

Relationships uncovered

If you want to succeed in long-term relationships:

- **don't skimp on the foreplay;**
- **have good intercourse;**
- **consider multiple climaxes over time;**
- **review performance in the cool of the afterglow – leave out the cigarette or picking your toenails; and**

- **remember: the sex analogy includes romance, love and friendship, not just scoring.**

Amazon are an excellent company who have the full cycle working for them. They have mastered online foreplay: you get exactly what you ask for, when you asked for it and they keep the relationship going by suggesting things you would like based on what you have previously bought. For example, if you bought a Madonna DVD last week, they will suggest possible purchases based on what their intelligence tells them about people like you. Since most of us are creatures of habit, many of their predictions are spot on. By the way, if you wish to screw their marketing strategy, adopt a systematically random lifestyle. Example: purchase toupees one week and shampoo the next! Amazon do not sell toupees as I write this, but you get the general idea ...

By contrast, another world-famous company have a dumb approach to online relationships – they seem keen to find ways to stop you buying stuff. One example comes from their online sales page, where they have found the ultimate way to turn new and existing customers off. If you try to buy products from them the first three questions they ask you run something like this:

1. Your name

2. Your shipping address

3. Your email address

All reasonable questions. But then Question 4 is rather sad:

4. Do you intend to use the product for terrorism? (YES or NO)?

Hardly a good chat-up line, nor is it likely to get you in the mood for a sale if you are an existing customer. Now, I think you all know why they ask Question 4, but why not ask you to tick a box to say you have read all the terms and conditions? Buried in the terms-and-conditions document on page 355 you would be asked if you were a terrorist, had thoughts of moral turpitude or had been a member of the Nazi party, and all the usual questions for covering themselves. Worse still, I've mailed this company several times about this but have had no response.

THE GOOD THE BAD & THE UGLY

in relationships

AMAZON COMPLETE THE RELATIONSHIP CYCLE: FOREPLAY, INTERCOURSE, CLIMAX AND AFTERGLOW.

THE OTHER WELL-KNOWN COMPANY OFFER LITTLE ONLINE FOREPLAY, APART FROM ASKING YOU IF YOU ARE A TERRORIST – HARDLY LIKELY TO GET YOU INTO BED WITH THEM.

1. Foreplay – Light my fire

Many books, numerous pages of graphics and mass debates have been filled with stuff about the importance of the psychological contract. The topic is crucial. After all, a good psychological contract accounts for most business success especially where supplier–purchaser or partnership arrangements are concerned. Many bad business relationships also have their root cause in a poorly made or broken psychological contract. If you've ever had a dose of 'Good Lovin' Gone Bad' at work or play, you'll know where I'm comin' from …

Despite its importance, some academics make the subject indigestible and meaningless. Simply stated, the psychological contract describes the unwritten parts of a relationship that make or break success. If you have time to attend two or three weeks at a business school, you might conclude that the psychological contract consists of the following things:

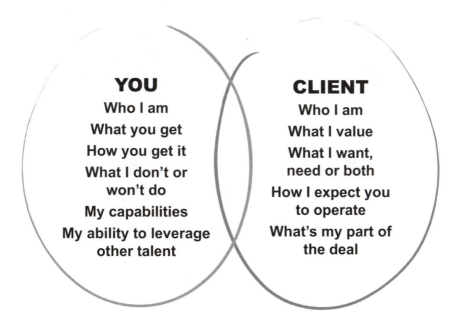

YOU
Who I am
What you get
How you get it
What I don't or
won't do
My capabilities
My ability to leverage
other talent

CLIENT
Who I am
What I value
What I want,
need or both
How I expect you
to operate
What's my part of
the deal

My contention is that most work relationships either never start or they break down, not because of what is promised, but because of what is implied but never discussed or agreed and then accidentally broken. Can we fix it? Let's see what the great and the good have to say about this:

What you learn about the psychological contract from the Academy of Rock

At the Academy of Rock, business jargon is replaced by five to ten words:

'I'd Do Anything for Love (But I Won't Do That)' – Meat Loaf's classic anthem shows the importance of the psychological contract (what's in and out of the relationship). We can only begin to imagine what the songwriter, Jim Steinman, may have had in mind by 'that' in the world of work – clients have ironically suggested 'that' means 'work in a call centre'. In business, the unspoken 'that' word contributes to the meltdown of most successful relationships. A lot of time is spent discussing what people will achieve together, but no time is spent on what's not in the deal.

For longer-lasting relationships, find out and agree what 'that' is, because they could be the unspoken elements that, if not addressed, will kill the relationship.

'Like a Virgin' – Madonna's famous hit reminds us of the need to treat every new relationship as though it were the first time. Also the need to refresh existing relationships. These are most often neglected out of familiarity. Eventually people notice that 'You Don't Bring Me Flowers Anymore' and dump us.

This happened with a university that used to have an excellent track record in staff relationships, which impacted positively on the way students were treated. It produced a real sense of belonging and above-the-line performance that went with it. However, the university broke the spell by reducing tutor roles to a series of transactional administrative tasks involving little or no human communication. As a result, people became demoralised. The best ones left, the students stopped behaving like an unpaid sales force and ceased referring new clients – which impacted on top and bottom lines. As punk rocker Ian Dury might have said, what a waste!

How can you make over existing relationships so that they feel brand new?

Simply the best bank?

First Direct Bank, part of HSBC, stand out from the crowd in their approach to client relationships. They redefine the meaning of 'distance' in banking, by providing intelligent telephone-banking staff who can read their clients, and who are supported by an effective intelligence system that allows each representative to treat clients personally. This is remarkable simply because many other banks have client knowledge systems at their disposal, but do not use the intelligence.

Any strategy that rests solely on functional value is risky in markets where products can be rapidly copied. The only service differentiator is the power of relationship. First Direct do it all – style and substance, head and heart, great business savvy, business sex without spillages … Of course, it's not raw sex: First Direct are the first romantic bank. Also a lot more sexy than traditional banks … Business gurus show a graphic at this point:

	Functional 'head' appeal	
High Emotional 'heart' appeal	Some e-banks with low back room functionality	First Direct
Low	Traditional banks	Banks with substance but no style
	Low High	

We saw the perils of style running ahead of substance when the UK Department of Trade and Industry (DTI) renamed itself the Department for Productivity, Energy and Industry (DPEI). Within minutes DPEI had come to stand for 'Dippy' and 'Penis'. Within hours the name was changed back to the DTI. DTI has a massive problem with the functional value of what it does: an ill-defined set of services and activities that overlap and contradict one another. A simple makeover of its name only served to emphasise perceptions that style matters more than substance.

Given that Amazon and First Direct are masters of foreplay, intercourse and so on, how does your business approach 'online sex'? How can you get romance, love and trust into the equation?

Name that tune?

Many rock songs are about relationships. We've translated a well-known one into its hidden meaning below. Just for the hell of it, have a look and see if you can guess the song title:

Two men had an intense bonding experience involving an animal early on in their careers. This experience produced an intensely strong psychological contract that would be tested later.

Many years on, they faced another critical challenge, again involving an animal. They remembered the earlier experience and copied the behaviour they had used at the time. However, the context for their behaviour was quite different. A different course of action would have been better, if only they had recognised the different circumstances.

The business lessons of the story are that:

The psychological contract is very hard to break if it's powerful.
Businesses need to work extremely hard to escape mental tramlines, especially where these have been laid down through high levels of experience and comfort with a particular business model.

So, can you guess what it is yet?

Find out on page 85.

Tuning into others

Most of the time, our relationships are based on discovering natural similarities, e.g. we like the same music, have common ambitions, share a liking for chocolate spread on our bodies etc. At work, however, we sometimes have to rub along with people whom we wouldn't share our house or underwear with. When we have no natural source of bondage, the discipline known as neuro-linguistic programming (NLP) informs us that rapport skills can be learned and enhanced. This builds on the fact that interpersonal communication is mostly influenced by the way we say things, not what we say. The more we are like someone else – in the way we are, how we communicate, both verbally and nonverbally – the more likely they will like us. In studies on communication, it was estimated that only 7% of communication is composed of the syntax we use, 38% our voice tone/tempo etc., and 55% our body language.

Ring my bell?

When you need to make a relationship work and there are no natural sources of rapport, simply match the other person's observable behaviour: the way they speak (the voice tone and quality, their rhythm and tempo – but not their accent), the language they use, their body language etc. This is not about mimicking but respecting their way of being. Leaders match others as a natural skill rather than as a 'sprayed-on method'. There are many ways to match other people – see below:

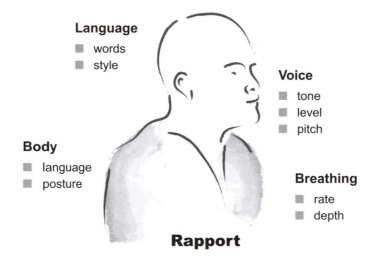

Language
- words
- style

Voice
- tone
- level
- pitch

Body
- language
- posture

Breathing
- rate
- depth

Rapport

The science of relationships

'Gravitation cannot be held responsible for people falling in love.'

Albert Einstein

'Physics is like sex: sure, it may give some practical results, but that's not why we do it.'

Richard Feynman, American Physicist

Just think about the phonology of communication. Some people speak a lot, some are loud, others quiet, some speak in a noticeable rhythm, others more staccato, some have an implicit structure to their conversation, others jam. The music and notes – the human dynamics – of communication are worth tuning into if you want to be more skilful in relationships.

Key point

If you wish to gain greater engagement with others, try noticing the music and notes of their conversation and join in with the flow. This is the skill that experienced musicians use in a jam session. We can learn lots about communication from music.

If you wish to disconnect from a communications sequence rapidly, try mismatching. This can be subtle as well as obvious.

Harmony

Some believe that NLP is so powerful that it presents ethical problems for leaders. Of course it is possible to use NLP in a shallow way as a tool of manipulation. NLP then stands for 'Now Let's Pretend'. However, it does not have to be like that. The difference between influence and manipulation is that manipulation is purely self-centred, whereas influence is self- *and* other-centred. One-sided approaches eventually pay the instigator back in the groin. NLP uses the term 'congruence' to indicate when behaviour is aligned with values. I prefer 'harmony', which can be both internal and external:

- *Inner harmony*: An absence of behaviour and value conflicts. In other words, all your outcomes fit together in a harmonious way. Lack of internal harmony is a principal reason why people decide not to follow objectives that have been imposed on them at work or give up bad habits such as smoking in bed or writing lengthy meeting minutes.

- *Outer harmony*: This is about aligning your outcomes with those of the other stakeholders involved in reaching a goal. One vision, one mission.

The science of relationships

'Love is a matter of chemistry, but sex is a matter of physics.'

Albert Einstein

Relax?

While you can use techniques for enhancing relationships, there is also room for doing what comes naturally and using your intuition and attitude. After all, the letters MBA stand for Management By Attitude rather than More Bloody Analysis. We live in a world where almost everything is analysed. A Financial Times survey revealed that 74% of respondents used intuition in relationships, 59% in business and 9% in investment decisions. This, of course, accounts for the huge sales of romantic novels and Harry Potter books to bank managers, accountants and stockbrokers …

To balance out paralysis by analysis and technique, you must learn to trust your intuition and attitude a little more. Smart people spend a lot of their time using lunch, hunch and basic instinct to inform decision making, and even more time trying to cover their decision processes up with logic, lest others discover that they had used a less robust method.

For example a social services leader came up with a remarkable idea to address a complex problem in child protection that had troubled people for ages without resolution. She presented the idea to her peers and seniors and it was warmly received. After the agreement to go forward had been made, someone casually asked how she came up with the idea. Seeing no reason to lie, she calmly said, 'Oh I thought of it while I was eating my cornflakes this morning.' Shock, horror! The mood of the meeting plummeted. After several hours of hand wringing, they decided that the idea could not be used without extensive research and pilot testing. Game over! The idea would have been acceptable if her intuitive answer had been masked with phrases such as 'focus group', 'benchmarking', and 'public consultation'. To them the intuitive truth was just unacceptable. Therefore I would argue that there is room for smiles, lies and faking it in order to live inside the expectations of others. This is a tough judgement call.

Where do you need to cover up intuitive leaps of faith, and where would it be better to deal in the truth as the Cornflake Girl did in our example?

Practical intuition

To develop intuition, play music, preferably blindfolded.

Wear ear plugs at your next meeting.

Use lunch, hunch and basic instinct more.

2. Intercourse – Good vibrations?

We now live in a world where we expect most things to go right. The last hundred years have seen many life-threatening diseases eradicated, a general speeding up in service delivery and a willingness to complain about what you get – whether or not the criticism is deserved. One consequence of this in the Western world is that many people expect to live in a society where everything goes according to *their* plan. Organisations can moan and bitch about this, but, in such a world, we must deliver products and services on a right-first-time basis. It also matters that they are served up in the right way. Good business intercourse is about delivering the promise: not only the journey but also the final outcome. Love is involved at the level of caring passionately about both doing the right things and doing them right. Some like it hot and fast; others slow and cool. We could go on to discuss special positions, the use of toys, STDs, contraception, Viagra, abstinence, S&M, 1:1 versus group sex, fetishes, whips, chains … But there isn't time now, so, instead, let me talk about unnatural bedfellows …

Loving the alien?

Opposites don't attract at work, even if they do in the home and in bed (but sometimes desire spills over into the workplace – see story opposite). Although it is likely that you surround yourself with agreeable people at work, it is a pity that agreeable people do not ask each other challenging questions, do not generally have a diverse skillset, and dare not venture into unknown territories. Rock groups have difference, diffidence and dissonance built into them as a design principle. The singer is a different animal from the shy drummer, yet they must work together if they are to rock. I am not saying that it's easy playing in a band. But, then, whoever said that it had to be easy? In life, as in a rock band, there are frequent conflicts. Therefore, wise companies welcome conflict by ensuring that there is a rich mixture of people, and that these are mixed up in different permutations from time to time. This is different from sticking diversity posters on the wall, using the Village People teamwork strategy (you will recall that the disco sensation the Village People had a cowboy, an Indian, a construction worker, a cop and so on in the band) or including a token minority person in every team.

Broom cupboards, whips, skips and biochemistry

Scientists are great experimenters and given the right circumstances will extend their curiosity to less familiar areas such as relationships. I recall a time in the drug company I worked for, when two research-and-development scientists were caught having sex in the broom cupboard during their tea break. This caused great amusement when the cleaning lady caught them straddling the industrial vacuum cleaner. Do you have that picture clear in your mind yet?

I also worked with a blond-haired biologist who had an annoyingly good reputation with women. A fresh female pharmacist arrived in the lab, and created an immediate stir by putting a bullwhip up above her desk and bragging about how big her bike was. Needless to say, this drew the biologist's attention. Pheromones were exchanged and, shortly after, they let slip that they had been copulating in an empty waste-disposal skip. As a result of this, the pharmacist acquired the name Skippy after the famous TV kangaroo. Anyway, back to the broom cupboard …

The broom-cupboard incident prompted a lengthy series of meetings in HR. These revolved around the process (whether it was OK to have sex at break time; was break time part of work or play?) rather than the outcome (whether any scientific breakthroughs had been made as a result of the endorphin release). Hands were wrung, brows mopped furiously. Some of the HR people wanted to know what sex in a broom cupboard might be like; others were just curious about what sex might be like. It was finally decided to move one of the chemists half a mile to another building, to reduce the CPR (Copulation Probability Ratio). This simple action was enough to hold back the possibility of IDCF (Inter-Discipline Cross-Fertilisation) for some years to come …

The moral of this story is that passion is vital for peak performance. Passion can also be of the mental variety and it can be directed towards business goals rather than self-gratification. So, no excuses for sex with industrial vacuum cleaners in skips …

It takes two?

George Michael sums up teamwork in the chorus of the classic Wham song 'I'm Your Man'. He sings, 'If you're gonna do it, do it right.' The word 'it' is unspecified, just as 'that' is in Meat Loaf's song. In the business world, I reckon 'it' means:

> *If we're going to work in cross-discipline teams, we had better implement the process correctly, through genuinely valuing diversity, daring to challenge norms and learning from success and failure.*

These could be the words of a song in a concept album by an esoteric rock group, such as Yes, but they ain't Rock'n'Roll because they don't scan.

Pairs and teams are vital for innovation in 21st century businesses because innovation is so complex that it's rare for all the relevant talents to reside in one person. Although it is known that good teams come up with fewer ideas than individuals do, these ideas are often better developed and more doable than those produced by lone geniuses. Musical pairs are a common combination for creativity and innovation. Just think of the following 'duos': Lennon and McCartney; Carpenter and Carpenter; Lennox and Stewart; Watson and Crick; Rogers and Hammerstein; Jagger and Richard; Otway and Holgarth; the Cocteau Twins … The business world understands and agrees with the power of duos and teams.

Oticon, the Swedish hearing-aid company, understand how to make differences work to advantage in business. They have an uncompromising attitude to selecting staff who are prepared to challenge everything. They work in multifunctional teams put together in order to bring different abilities to bear on producing the world's best hearing devices. The CEO, Lars Kolind, believes that you cannot have an intelligent company if you try to run it using the command-and-control model. Instead, he suggests we should grow up and treat the company as though it had a collective brain. Read all about Oticon at www.oticon.com and in *Karaoke Capitalism* by Rock'n'Roll professors Kjell Nordström and Jonas Ridderstråle.

Village People?

Bands are excellent examples of what on paper should be a completely dysfunctional team. They are often composed of completely different types, sometimes held together only by a love for what they do or because the band manager somehow keeps the show on the road and stops fights. Let's look at the worst stereotypes to see if you can identify analogies in the crazy world of work.

- The bassist is usually morose and depressive – perhaps clinically so. Often late, fairly uncommunicative, they gain pleasure from setting their equipment up first and then heading for the bar. They often despise the lead guitarist for reasons of taste and dress sense.

- The drummer will be as mad as a loon. But you have to put up with them, otherwise the band disintegrates. This means letting the drummer perform a song they wrote while on drugs even though it's rubbish. There are two sorts of drummer: the extrovert ones such as Keith Moon; and the more usual shy drummers. I once worked with one in a punk band who was so shy that he insisted on playing behind a screen!

- What matters most to the lead guitarist is whether they have a fan (mechanical or human) in front of them to make them look cool, while playing endless solos. I work with some of these guys at jam sessions in my spare time. They waste electricity and oxygen, and don't contribute to the overall direction. I am a lead guitarist, so I know what I'm talking about!

- The singer's main concerns are about the lighting, whether the fans (human) can see them and how many people they will have sex with that night.

Does your business have the right balance of musicians for the music it plays? Who is in your fan club? How does the fan club assist your business?

What can we learn about teams from the gurus?

Bruce Tuckman suggested that teams go through four stages of development: forming, storming, norming and performing. In the context of continuous change, I'd add a fifth stage: re-forming.

Forming

The team is a collection of individuals at this point. People talk about purpose, identity, composition. Individuals are usually keen to make an impression on the team at this stage, but may not take that many real risks. Nobody mentions the need for a common purpose, let alone shared processes, Post-it notes, uniforms or toys.

Storming

After an initial superficial consensus, most teams go through a period of conflict. At this stage, the purpose, leadership and other roles, working patterns and the behaviour of the team and its members may all be challenged. As personal agendas may be revealed, conflict is to be expected. The storming stage is vital for the formation of trust within the team. The attempt to put a lid on conflict rarely works and it is better to deal with it properly. If storming is successfully handled, the team will move on to the next stage.

The storming process can take minutes or years. Some rock bands go through the entire cycle in one evening. On other occasions the standard recipe for getting rid of the weakest band member is to break up one week, then re-form the band the next, without the unwanted member. The Beatles offer us an interesting viewpoint on longer-term teamwork. We'll look at this next.

What can we learn about teams from the Academy of Rock?

With The Beatles – Teamwork in action

Stage 1 – The Forming Stage
1957 to 1960 – from Liverpool to Hamburg

Stage 2 – The Storming Stage
1961 to 1962 – from Hamburg to The Cavern

Stage 3 – The Norming Stage
1961 to 1962 – the Cavern Club, Brian Epstein, George Martin and Ringo

Stage 4 – The Performing Stage
1963 to 1967 – the Fab Four and Beatlemania

Stage 5 – The Re-forming Stage or Break-Up
1967 to 1970 – the death of Brian Epstein, Apple and the Fab Fallout.

John MacCarfrae uses The Beatles as a compelling metaphor to develop teams. A native of Liverpool, John is uniquely positioned to offer us lessons in teamwork from The Beatles.

The long and winding road

Knowing how goals and roles fitted into the bigger picture enabled The Beatles to behave effectively without having everything spelled out in such detail that it became restrictive. Believing that their roles were equally important, knowing how they related to the whole, and having a reasonable fit between their personal goals and the band's goals energised and motivated John, Paul, George and Ringo to have seventeen Number 1 hits in the UK.

Norming

The team establishes norms and patterns of work under which it will operate, e.g. how it should work, how decisions are taken, how open it can be. There will be much tentative experimentation by people who are testing feelings and opinions within the team and establishing their level of commitment.

Performing

Only when the other three stages are complete will the team be fully productive.

The time and effort required to go through the four stages depends on the circumstances facing the team. Teams get stuck at particular stages and may return to earlier stages as new challenges are faced. The cycle is not a one-off event. Teams may return to forming at each meeting, depending on the level of cohesion arising from previous meetings.

Re-forming

When the team's purpose is over, there is a need to regroup and start over. However, if things have gone well, dismantling a successful team can be harder than starting one up because there is now a solid bond between the team members. Some people call this stage 'mourning', because it resembles what happens when people suffer a loss. Sometimes a symbolic ritual is needed to recognise the team's contribution and to close down its formal business together.

Know what stage you are at and watch out for the early warning signs of regression or break-up.

You cannot cheat the cycle by trying to jump stages. You can, however, anticipate the stages and do the right things at the right times, thus moving the team on.

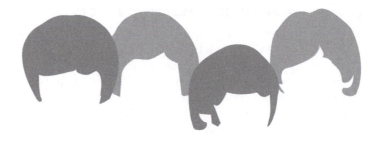

Come together

Few things are more discouraging than being a part of a dysfunctional team. It's difficult to put forth your best effort when other team members don't support each other, don't follow through on commitments and don't stick by the decisions the team has made. Team members need to know one another at a deeper level than the role each is playing. This tends to generate a genuine interest in each other's individual success, and, in the final analysis, is essential for excellent cooperation. Making and using ground rules greatly improves teamwork by improving team action and interaction.

Getting better

The Beatles made being creative an everyday part of their work. Being more creative means working smarter and having more fun. The *Sgt. Pepper* years were a testimony to this philosophy. However, it meant investing the time and effort to explore new frontiers, considering new points of view and creating new mental runways.

Revolution

The Beatles were one of the greatest teams ever in the history of popular music. The main reason for the eventual break-up in 1970 was complacency and a failure to address important team issues that were a prerequisite for their continuing success. From 1968, they went into a decline that they were unable to halt. Maintaining such a high level of success is tough when team members begin to have hidden agendas, selfish motives or conflicting goals. The roadblocks, bottlenecks and problems that created dissatisfaction among John, Paul, George and Ringo were never addressed. By April 1970, it was all over.

Group sex – making partnerships work

Rather than using mergers and acquisitions as a means of gaining access to additional capabilities, a looser way of getting these benefits is to form partnerships. Unfortunately, many partnerships become more complicated than the problems they intend to solve, such as some of the public–private partnerships in the UK. The partnership process is somewhat like a naïve orgy: no one knows what the others want, and no one bothers to ask; there is much fumbling and frothing and nobody asks, 'How was it for you?' In the rock biz, the formation of supergroups is just as troublesome:

- there are usually too many experts – often guitarists;
- most supergroups end up playing mediocre songs; and
- supergroups rarely last very long.

So what separates the sheep from the goats in this field? Let's get serious for a moment.

The word 'partnership' has multiple meanings in today's business world. Meanings range from:

A deep and long-lasting relationship where the business's value-creating systems are joined in a way that enhances opportunity for both parties.

Or, more cynically:

A new way of dumping risk.

The second definition leads to a low-level relationship with lack of responsibility on both sides, as neither side has any commitment to the achievement of real value. So what are the hallmarks of successful partnerships?

Rock'n'Roll
PARTNERSHIPS

The formation of supergroups is usually troublesome and short-lived:

■ **too many experts spoil the broth; and**

■ **most supergroups end up playing pretty mediocre songs.***

*Listen to these supergroups, if you must, to hear this point:
Blind Faith
The Traveling Wilburys
Emerson, Lake and Palmer

Width is important? – Broaden the measures

One of the partners may have more clout and as a result always gets a larger share of the rewards. Just the same problem as men arguing over the size of their penis. Exxon seem to agree with this point, as they believe that most companies waste time, money and effort haggling over prices. This leads to continuous negotiations by people in both firms, causing internal combustion – heat without light. Ultimately, this drives out the possibility of reaching options that create real value for both sides over the long-term. Exxon's strategy is to focus on global goals where all can win.

Distinguish performance and relationship

Skilled partnership brokers make a clear distinction between the elements of a deal that drive performance (not only carrots but also sticks) and those elements that build the relationship (not only glue but also lubricant). Perhaps this is the difference between worrying about how many positions you and your partner can get into and then forgetting to clean up afterwards.

Kodak and IBM show how these drivers work in practice:

- **Performance drivers**: hardware retirement and replacement; use of third-party software; service levels; maintenance and security of data; pricing; employment transfer terms.
- **Relationship drivers**: reliability; giving each other the benefit of the doubt; no coercion; understanding each other's objectives; timeliness of consultations; mutual respect.

How do you glue your partners to you? How do you lubricate them so that they can do their best without having to adopt the irrelevant constraints of your business processes?

Partnerships as marriages

'Because of the trust and respect we've built up, like an old married couple, we are able to rubbish each other's ideas. Yes, we have to kill our babies – it's the only way to arrive at a viable idea.'

Simon Kershaw
creative director responsible for marketing the Land Rover Discovery

(Author's note: In this context, 'babies' are ideas!)

Getting better – Building in continuous improvement

It's foolish to assume that a partnership will be a right-first-time affair, even after a honeymoon period. There are two contracts in play:

1. *The written contract*: Overzealous contract managers, aided and abetted by corporate lawyers, have turned these into at least a 200-page art form.

2. *The psychological contract*: Best described as how each party will respond to a critical incident (good, bad or ugly). We looked at this on pages 45-5.

We know from the music business that the written contract is good only for settling disputes – it does very little for improving performance. Yet frequently people use the written contract as the only instrument of partnership or domination. A consequence is that the partnership must be reviewed on a regular basis. A useful format for this is:

What's working?	How can we expand or improve this?
What's not working?	How can we modify or eliminate this?

D.I.V.O.R.C.E. – Know the exit criteria

It's wise to specify conditions under which the partnership will end and what this will mean. In practice, this includes who gets what under a variety of circumstances, for example, if the marketing plan fails. A failure to specify these elements can result in disastrous consequences. There was extended legal wrangling after The Beatles split up, and also to a lesser degree after Mick and Bianca Jagger separated.

Good relationships require us to be persuasive in our communications. We'll look at this next ...

Breaking up is hard to do

John Lennon and Paul McCartney were quite different as individuals, but managed to respect rather than reject each other's differences for many years.

Eventually, these differences became a weakness rather than strengths. Many partnerships undergo the same transformation.

How can you spot and stop the rot?

Persuasive communication

Persuasive communication is all about getting other people to do something that you want. In rock music we want people to dance, get excited and buy the records. In business, we want staff to comply or commit to what the enterprise is all about. Easier said than done. If I had a dollar for every business that said they had communication problems, I would be able to retire. So how exactly can we improve the way we communicate? Do staff need to spend more time in bars? Is the business structured in silos that prevent people cross-pollinating (or cross-dressing, a.k.a. job swaps)? Is a professional dating service required on the HR website? Communication is simple in theory, but the other person may be using a different theory. The business school answer to the problem is shown below:

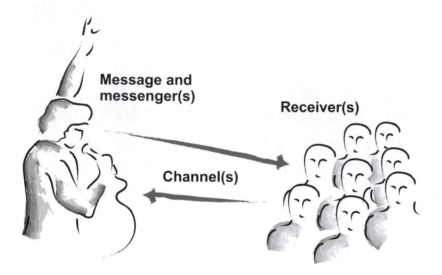

If you had only a minute to talk about persuasive communication, you would say:

- Ensure that the message is clear and potent. It needs to be couched in terms that the receivers will understand, accept and act upon.
- Use messengers that will be heard and understood.
- Use media for the job that will be heard – a balance between the most effective and efficient routes, to target both head and heart.
- Ensure the receivers are engaged. This means picking the right time and place and ensuring that your message is not affected by noise or feedback in the system.

COMMUNICATION BREAKDOWN

TO UNDERSTAND HOW GOOD INTENTIONS PRODUCE UNEXPECTED OUTCOMES, BUY YOURSELF A COPY OF THE CLASSIC ROCKUMENTARY *THIS IS SPINAL TAP* AND WATCH THE 'STONEHENGE' SEQUENCE.

THIS IS NOT TOO DIFFERENT FROM THE WAY THAT BAD PROJECTS ARE MANAGED IN BUSINESS.

Easy to say of course. People are bombarded by persuasive communication, and making sure your message is heard above the noise and feedback of daily life requires considerable thought. Research on persuasive communication offers vital insights into what works. Let's take each element in turn.

The message

Does your message present a unique advantage compared with alternative ways of satisfying the need? This might be a single feature or a unique bundle of features that give it the wow factor. Once this is established, it needs to be converted into a form that others can understand and engage with. This means serving it up using the target audience's predominant thinking style(s). Recall the discussion about phonology of communications on page 50.

One-sided messages such as 'simply the best' work best when the receivers already agree with the argument, or when they are unlikely to hear counterarguments. Two-sided messages tend to be more effective when the receivers initially disagree with the argument, where they are well educated, or when they are likely to hear counterviews. It's better to draw conclusions rather than let others infer them for themselves. Repetition can increase persuasiveness (think about how chorus lines work in rock songs) but nagging can wear out a message. Repeating ideas rather than exact messages may be the best solution.

The messenger

Messengers are more influential when receivers think they have high credibility. Honesty and trustworthiness are also vital. Just think about how politicians crave these qualities. Therefore, a messenger's influence is weakened when the audience thinks it has something to gain from the communication. Bad salespeople have turned this into the phrase 'I'm not trying to sell you anything …', which usually means exactly the opposite. Expertise, status and positivity also help. People are persuaded more by communicators they perceive to be like themselves, which accounts for the number of corporate-style gurus in the business world these days.

Persuasive communication unplugged

Make your message clear and potent.

Use messengers that will be heard.

Use media for the job that will be heard.

Ensure the receivers are engaged

The receiver

Receivers need to be able to understand the message being sent. First of all there must be a perceived need, otherwise they will not want to know. For example, it is no good trying to persuade vegetarians that British Beef is Best.

If you wish to be more persuasive and already know your receivers, knowing some general personality traits will help your cause. People with low self-esteem tend to be more persuadable than those having high self-esteem. This does not mean that you need to crush anyone's feelings of self-worth before you attempt to persuade them! Anxious people are low in persuadability. How can you relax them with a first course as part of the foreplay before starting inter-course? People who are high in rich imagery, fantasies and dreams are more persuadable. This explains why S&M (sales & marketing) people are potentially easy sales targets! People of high general intelligence are more influenced by messages based on impressive logical arguments and are less likely to be influenced by messages with false, illogical or irrelevant arguments.

Generalisations are generally unhelpful. You must work within the specific realities of each situation, perhaps holding this wisdom as a set of heuristics or rules of thumb rather than absolute truths. Avoid being too dogmatic. It's far better to state your message in such a way that the receivers think that it's their own idea, so that they actually persuade themselves!

There are several types of receivers in any persuasive communication:

- **gatekeepers**: people who control the entry and exit points to the people who hold opinions and make decisions about your proposal;
- **influencers**: people who have wide networks and are the key opinion formers; and
- **decision makers**: people who make decisions to commit money, people and time to a proposal.

People waste a great deal of time asking the wrong questions of the wrong stakeholders. It's no use asking a gatekeeper to approve your proposal, nor is it always useful to ask a decision maker for their opinion of the technical merits of a proposal. It could even backfire on your strategy by putting them in a place of discomfort.

DANGEROUS LIAISONS

'ALL GREAT IDEAS ARE DANGEROUS.'
OSCAR WILDE

SO HOW CAN YOU MAKE
THEM SAFE FOR THOSE WHO NEED
TO BE PERSUADED?

The medium

There are a multitude of communication media available: face-to-face, email, memos, presentations, focus groups, the grapevine, advertisements, notice boards, text messages, faxes, the press, TV, radio, CD, DVD and so on.

If you are trying to persuade someone of the value of an untested concept or a fragile new idea in business, it is more often the case that you will be dealing with individuals or small groups of people. In such circumstances the list of media narrows down to two-way communication media rather than one-way transmission media such as TV. In general, media that use face-to-face contact are much better for persuading people, as they allow for a dialogue rather than a monologue. However, such media are expensive in time and the skills needed. It is tempting to use media such as email for persuasion since they are very efficient. However, email is not always an effective persuasive medium, since it makes it very easy for the receivers to reject your proposal. Research indicates that introvert male executives in particular spend a great deal of time crafting responses to emails if they wish to reject an idea or criticise it in some way. This is less possible during hand-to-hand combat.

If you wish to be persuasive, the less efficient media are often more effective. Persuasive people spend more time on the phone and in hand-to-hand combat than they do on email and using the joy of text.

H1T ME W1TH YOUR RHYTHM ST1CK

Don't dance to the rhythm.
Change it.

Or use the rhythm method.

Getting down and dirty – Dealing with politics

Businesses are not machines. They are communities of people, and therefore behave just like other communities. Politics is a feature of most businesses. People compete among themselves for power and resources; there are differences of opinion and of values, conflicts of priorities and of goals. To assume that your business is free of power differences is to accept that you are likely to be only 50 per cent effective, since you are dealing with only the rational part of life in business. You must be able to deal with the 'dark side of the force' to be an effective leader. The choices that are available reduce to the punk rock song 'Should I Stay or Should I Go?'. More subtle versions of this song include:

- Should I stay and contribute? This can be seen as loyalty, or pragmatism.
- Should I go? Effectively, 'I'm taking my marbles and going.'
- Should I stay and try to change the system?

Those who stay and try to change the system have two choices:

- work as **conformist innovators**, accepting the dominant values and relationships within the business and attempting to demonstrate how their activities contribute to the organisation's success criteria;
- become **deviant innovators** and, by working towards organisational success in their own way, demonstrate that their contributions provide a different yet better set of criteria for change, thereby gaining acceptance of their ideas.

Given that politics are a fact of life, it's best to be aware of the different types of games out there, so that you can deal with them in the best way.

'Only free men can negotiate. Prisoners
cannot enter into contracts.'

Nelson Mandela

Dance with the devil – Political games

Political games involve illegitimate use of power, but many use legitimate authority as part of the play. The main games are:

Games to resist authority

Insurgency: Shafting your superiors. Oddly enough, this is good for high performance if used in moderation and for a good enough reason.

Games to counter resistance

Counterinsurgency: Shafting yourself through more rules, regulations and punishments. Generally counterproductive for a high-performance business.

Games to build power bases

Bondage: Attaching oneself to a useful superior or star player. Healthy if the purpose is harmonious for you and the business.

Run with the pack: Forming a peer network. You can spot this when interest groups or committees spring up around new ideas for no obvious good reasons. May be necessary if your business or national culture exhibits high power distance, as Dutch guru Geert Hofstede would describe it.

The empire strikes back: Building coalitions of subordinates. There isn't always safety in numbers. Beware those people who say 'I'm right behind you.' Invariably, when you need them, quite surprisingly they are not and have frequently developed collective amnesia at this point.

Money, money, money: Getting control of resources. As Prince says, 'Money don't buy you happiness, but it sho' 'nuff pays for the ride.' An extreme example of controlling resources came from a prison where staff were allowed free use of the photocopier but the boss locked up all the paper.

Lessons from the dark side...

'An eye for an eye only ends up making the whole world blind.'

Mahatma Gandhi

Bigger brain: Flaunting and feigning expertise. Can be spotted when people mention their titles or greater knowledge on a consistent basis with no obvious reason for this behaviour. Can backfire if the expertise is not as genuine or the cause is not worth it. In any case, when the going gets tough, brains are usually defeated by brawn.

Bigger title: Flaunting one's authority. Akin to having large sexual parts – as we all know, size frequently disappoints, so, as Pink Floyd might have said, 'Careful with that long title, Eugene …'

Games to defeat rivals

War of the Worlds: The line-versus-staff game, played between units or functions, where people use power vested in functional units to over-power arguments for doing things across the business. This can lead to the breakdown of long-term relationships and destroys the trust needed for the business to flourish.

Games to change the company

This town ain't big enough for the both of us: As Sparks might have said, informing on an opponent. This may be efficient but is sure to destroy the climate for high performance and risk taking in the future. It's not therefore always effective.

We shall overcome: Mobilising enclaves of key rebels. Often visible through the formation of innovation clubs and in a more benign way through suggestions schemes. Some companies encourage this strategy deliberately as a means of increasing innovation levels in the business.

Games, used in moderation, can have a healthy effect on keeping your business on its toes. A little sand in your joints is good for performance. Carried too far or done for the wrong reasons, however, political games turn the whole business into a political cauldron and divert it from its main task.

Games without frontiers –
Manipulation the Rock'n'Roll way

Madonna rocketed to stardom so quickly in 1984 that it obscured most of her musical virtues. Appreciating her music became even more difficult later on as her lifestyle became more of a talking point than her music. However, Madonna manipulated the media and the public with her music, her videos, her publicity and her sexuality. Arguably, Madonna was the first female pop star to have complete control of her music and image. Whether we approve of her means, we can't deny that she has made a huge impact on the world. Britney Spears and a host of others have learned much from Madonna.

3. Climax – Stairway to heaven, or take the lift?

Sex loses some of its metaphorical powers here, but what the hell! Nobody said the world was perfect, so I'll carry on. This is because, at work, we don't just want our Customers, Clients and Colleagues to have one orgasm. We're looking for multiple occurrences over time to keep them interested. In this context, the predominantly male idea of reaching a single climax (and then falling asleep) has limited application – in the way that many sales people think of the idea of closing a sale. Imagine how you would feel if you were sold something and immediately told that the salesperson was now going to have a fag (that's a cigarette, for our US readers).

The real question is, how do you build energy and excitement for what you have to offer your clients, be they purchasers of a product or consumers of a service, private or public? Does your product or service benefit from delayed gratification and a slow build-up, or are your customers the 'I want it all, and I want it now' types?

Faking it?

There is a huge currency in faking it at work. Some people are prepared to deceive colleagues in order to avoid discomfort and disagreements. This costs vast sums of money through the time wasted when people ask you to do things that subsequently are not required. However, there is a significant cost to authenticity versus bending the truth in order to preserve a relationship. Recall the Cornflake Girl story on page 52.

What can be done about this? The political-correctness pendulum has swung far too far at this current time. Of course, it will swing back in the way that ladies' hemlines move up and down with the whims of fashion, fans and fads. In the meantime, some of us may be content to gild the lily if we are to keep work relationships on an even keel.

Not faking it

Political correctness and creativity are
not good bedfellows.

If you want to run an innovative business, bring back
humour, irony, realism while maintaining respect.

If you want more creative ideas in your
company, get rid of the 'naughty thought police'
and introduce 'naughty rhythms'.

At the same time, know the difference
between 'sexist' and 'sexy'.

Orgasm addict

Can we become addicted to supreme service delivery? Of course we can. The problem comes when we're addicted to doing the same thing and the customer wants something different. What are the vital signs that let us know we need to vary the experience long before the customer has become dissatisfied and gone off somewhere else? Customers are promiscuous, some of them won't tell you that they are having an affair with a competitor and that they don't like you biting their ear while you are delivering their strategy workshops …

You can spot the early-warning signals that tell you it's time to change what you offer by tuning into people's unspoken needs. Neuro-linguistic programming calls this 'sensory acuity'. Musicians call it tuning in and turning on. First Direct calls it paying attention and reading the clients' minds. Recall that they are perhaps the first romantic bank in the world, against a backdrop of competitors that are neither sexy nor loving. Back to that graphic:

Once they have a good rapport with you – and, if they detect you are not in a hurry – they will use your phone call to find out about your unspoken needs. To do this, their frontline staff must be the most savvy people in the company. They don't rely on just the phone these days – if you want a quickie with no fuss, you can get on the Internet and do the functional stuff.

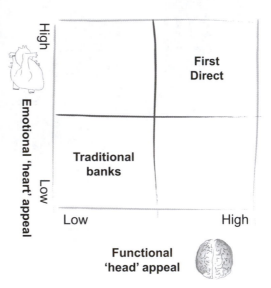

Find out if people want something different before it's too late. If you have invested time in a caring relationship, you can simply ask them.

Double Double
Pleasure Pleasure

'I became a schizophrenic
(so I could love you
twice).'

Tina C
www.tinac.net

Answer to the 'Name that tune?' item on page 47: 'Two Little Boys', as performed by Rolf Harris, the all-round Australian entertainer with multiple intelligences.

4. Afterglow – Will you still love me tomorrow?

It's one thing satisfying your Customers, Clients and Colleagues, it's another thing keeping them wanting more. In this context, what happens afterwards is what counts. Most businesses want to know the answer to the eternal question, 'Will you still love me tomorrow?'

The best some businesses can do after a sale is to ask the client, 'Can we put you on our Customer Relationship Management (CRM) database, so that we can send you a monthly newsletter and text updates about our innovative products and services?' Whoever wanted to hear that after an orgasm!? Let's face it: it's absurd, so just say no.

What you do want to know is something about the client experience, so that you can learn from it and build that into your competitive intelligence. Not many people like asking such questions in case the client did not like the experience, or, worse still, you didn't.

Talking this around with female friends and colleagues, I have been told that the way to solve the problem of a longer-lasting relationship comes down to some well-known, simple but rarely used methods:

- refreshing the sex – trying it on the kitchen table / booking a hotel for a weekend;
- introducing unusual moments of romance, love and friendship – 'moments of pleasure', as Kate Bush would have said;
- starting over – making sure each time is like the first time;
- fidelity – a.k.a. single-supplier agreements; and
- spicing things up with infidelity – a.k.a. competitive tendering.

Do any of these sound familiar to your customer relationship or marketing people? Which ones could you add to the mix?

Things you wish your Customers, Clients and Colleagues wouldn't say to you about you or your business

Did I shave my legs for this?

If love were oil, I'd be a quart low.

YES, YES, YES (when they actually mean NO, NO, NO).

Women fake orgasms, men fake relationships.

I still miss my wife, but my aim is improving.

You don't bring me flowers any more.

Summary

If you want to succeed in long-term relationships: don't skimp on the foreplay; have good intercourse; consider multiple climaxes over time; review performance in the cool of the afterglow. Stay awake! No need for a fag!

To improve relationships, try a little tenderness by matching people's body language. Within a loving relationship there is always the opportunity for using your intuition alongside technique, so be yourself – and let your partners be themselves – because you never know where that may lead!

You can learn lots about the power of diverse teams from music. At work you have to get along with people you might not choose as your sleeping partners. Music is a good model of making diversity work. There may be trouble ahead, though, so learn how to cope with dramas.

If you operate in a climate of politics, know the games, when to play them and the antidotes to unhealthy games.

Questions to ask back at the ranch

Three sets of questions to pose next time you're on stage:

1. What turns your customers on about what you do? Why do some of them want it all the time and why do others have less of an appetite for what you do?

2. How can you improve the effectiveness of your communication? How could you upgrade the quality of the message? What factors would influence your choice of the right medium and messengers? How could you ensure that the receivers are on your wavelength, and will engage with you? How good are your chat-up lines?

3. Which games should you stop playing in your business? Which games should you start? How might you begin the process of ridding yourself of the games that damage your business?

Dialogue 2

Drugs

**Rock on ...
Motivation and
Leadership**

When we deal with drugs in this part of the book, I'm not advocating that you take speed to run your business faster. Nor is there any need to smoke opium to help rewrite your mission statement in rhyming couplets that are much better than 'To be the first-choice supplier of products and expertise in our chosen markets through leveraged intelligence, bespoke solutions …' and so on, however worthy this might be. In my experience, people on drugs think they're really interesting, but to the outside world they're just people on drugs. As with our use of 'sex', I simply want to push your thinking in ways that business school gurus cannot. So we are talking adrenaline and endorphins here rather than crack and cocaine.

The drug analogy offers us some new definitions for familiar things:

'Drugging yourself' = Motivation – What gets you up really early in the morning? What turns you on at work? Where do you get your natural highs from? Are you part of the caffeine culture or a yoga obsessive? How can you release your creativity without smoking cannabis and forgetting what you thought afterwards? What is the motivational balance between your internal chemistry and the external stimuli? How can you make your work addictive? And so on.

'Drugging other people' = Leadership – I don't mean getting people to follow a blind (or blond) ambition. Academics discuss corporate culture as 'shared hallucinations about the way we do things around here' – that's a cult. I'm talking about pressing the magic buttons that get staff to work harder, smarter and longer than the rest of the world. How can you engage people in a collective ambition? How can you engender the kind of followers that will tell you that you are wrong before it's too late? What can we learn by contrasting what the great and the good say about these topics with the 6M Corporation hall of fame, i.e. Morrison, Morrissey, Morissette, Moby, Madonna, Marc Bolan, M People etc.? Two more Ms this time? Anyway, let's see.

CHOOSE LIFE

GEORGE MICHAEL ON WORK–LIFE BALANCE

George Michael advised us to 'enjoy what you do' in his 1982 hit 'Wham Rap'.

This is the ultimate recipe for synthesising your work with your life.

Later on, Wham's management produced T-shirts with 'Choose Life' on them. This was at least as influential as an MBA in helping me to leave a well-paid job and start a successful business from scratch twelve years ago.

Forget those 200-page self-help books on creating work–life balance. Decide what you want from life and then JFDI (Just Forget the past and Do It).

Motivation, a.k.a. drugging yourself

What makes you passionate? What gets you mad? What gets you out of bed in the morning wanting to do whatever it takes to succeed? What rocks your world? Can it be bottled? Is the pharmaceutical industry selling it yet? Has the government imposed regulations on it?

These are the kinds of questions that have occupied management gurus for nearly a century. You get very different answers to the questions depending on whom you ask. Let's compare the business guru answers with those from the Academy of Rock.

What you learn about motivation at business school

The acid test as to whether you have been successful in motivating somebody else is when they confidently say:

I KNOW   I CAN   I WILL

There are plenty of people out there who know loads of things and have great ability. People who are willing to apply their know-how and skill are a rare breed. In the words of the seventies West Coast (Wales, that is) acid rockers Man: 'Many are called but few get up.' There's nothing as practical as a good theory, so let's look at the classics:

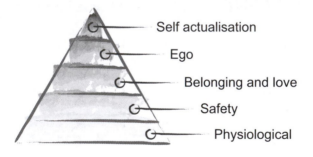

Maslow suggested a hierarchy of needs, which people try to meet through work, ranging from physiological needs (food and shelter) to self-actualisation (the need a person has to fulfil their potential). Maslow said that, given the chance, people attempt to harmonise their own goals with those of the enterprise. Maslow's triangle assumes that everyone has some sense of what they want from life. This tends to work in certain professions, for example, with doctors and teachers and with individuals who have a strong sense of purpose, such as those who pursue voluntary work.

What you learn about motivation at the Academy of Rock

'Heaven knows I'm miserable now'

The Smiths

Stephen Patrick Morrissey knows the perils of not making an active career choice. In The Smiths' song, 'Heaven Knows I'm Miserable Now', Morrissey discusses the problem of looking for a job and then just taking whatever you are offered as a recipe for disaster. Listen to this song or anything else Morrissey or The Smiths have written to reveal sharp-witted insights into Human Relations, the Universe and Everything.

The Tubes, a New York cult punk group, provided us with a quintes-sentially cynical viewpoint about mass consumption in their 1975 song, 'What Do You Want from Life?' In doing so, they logged the myriad de-sires, aspirations and fantasies that many people believe they should gain from employment. Check out their cult album *The Tubes* and listen to the rant at the end of this track.

The combined wisdom of the Gurus of Business with the Metal Gurus of Rock leads us to some practical conclusions:

- It's no good offering a teetotaller a bottle of whisky as an inducement. As Aretha Franklin and IBM said, 'Think'. In spite of organisational inconvenience, you need to customise recognition systems and rewards to self-actualised individuals, because if you do not engage their hearts and souls they will simply walk out of your doors.

- Work out what you want from work and life and devise a strategy to get it. Some might say you can't always get what you want, but sometimes you get what you need. So be focused and flexible and enjoy the surprises along the way.

Can't get no?

By contrast, Fred Herzberg picked out two different sets of factors that influence motivation and demoralisation at work. He called the first set of factors 'satisfiers' and the second 'dissatisfiers'. He said that the presence of dissatisfiers would cause loss of motivation but no amount of improvement in these factors would elicit positive motivation – this could only come from the thoughtful implementation of satisfiers at work. Satisfiers tend to be associated with self-actualisation needs, such as achievement, recognition, the work itself, responsibility, advancement. Dissatisfiers tended to be about environmental issues such as pay, working conditions, company policy and administration, supervision, a lack of recognition and advancement.

Herzberg's theories have largely stood the test of time, probably because they make sense. Asked the question, 'Why can't you get no satisfaction?', most people's answers line up with his theory.

What do I get?

Our third oldie but goldie is expectancy theory, proposed by Victor Vroom – or, as the Buzzcocks summed it up, 'What do I get?' This examines motivation in terms of the relationships between personal beliefs and expectations, effort, performance and outcomes. In other words:

- Is it possible to do it at all?
- Can I personally do it?
- Is it worth doing?
- What are the consequences?

The expectancy model is outlined opposite. Outcomes are classified as either *extrinsic*, in other words, outside yourself, such as pay, status both inside and outside work, fringe benefits, time off and praise from others, or *intrinsic*, in other words, more inner-directed things, which arise directly from the performance of the work, such as a sense of achievement, feelings of having done something worthwhile, self-respect and so on. Some people crave more external things, others internal. Key questions:

- What is your preference?
- Have you got the balance right?

Motivation unplugged

Expectancy theory in theory

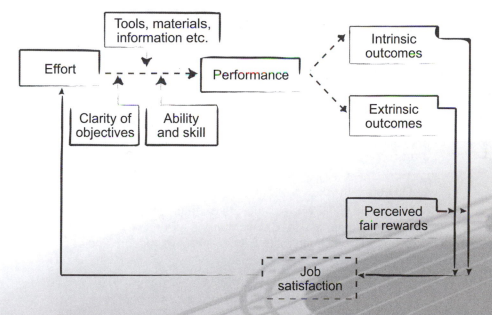

Expectancy theory in practice

Some of the links are probabilistic – indicated by the dotted lines. This means that there may be no easily perceivable relationship between effort and performance and outcomes. If the connection cannot be made, many people will not expend effort, as they don't think it's worthwhile or cannot see what's in it for them. This is the basic reason why many appraisal systems linked to pay do not work.

Is your appraisal system the Road to Motivational Hell or a Stairway to Performance Heaven?

The Road to Motivational Hell?

We learn well from best practice – see the Prêt à Manger example opposite. We can also learn an awful lot from bad practice. Finding examples of bad practice is usually easy. Look at the BBC's BPR initiative. I'm sure you know that the business jargon BPR stands for Business Process Re-Engineering. In this case, however, BPR refers to an altogether different process known as Biscuit Paradigm Retribution. This is where someone in the BBC noticed that the annual bill for biscuits was around half a million pounds. Now it takes a lot of time to eat that amount of biscuits! So, to implement cost savings, biscuits were struck from the corporate culture – which took the metaphorical and literal biscuit. A competitor CEO said at the time, 'It will be the worst half a million pounds he has ever saved.' The amount of wasted time BBC staff spent moaning about the biscuit cuts easily outweighed the biscuit bill. However, there is no column for 'corporate indigestion' on the balance sheet.

What can we learn from our tour of what the great, good and down-and-out offer us on motivation?

1. Motivation has never been a one-size-fits-all application. As more people head-butt the top of Maslow's triangle, they seek personalised answers to the question, 'Why should I work harder?' A simple reward system may serve HR's desire to do less work, but it will not create the conditions where people want to stay with you.

2. There is no point in trying to motivate a status-conscious extrovert with inner peace. Unless there is a Porsche on the lawn, they will not be interested. Apply Vroom's wisdom and act accordingly.

3. Rather than guess, ask your staff what they want from work/life.

4. Assess the cost of corporate indigestion before you remove the digestive biscuits!

What you learn about motivation at the Academy of Rock

I want it all (and I want it now)

We live in a consumption culture where mass individualism rules. Yet many companies still have only one way of rewarding people for their efforts. Get real, get a life and start making meaningful choices. Reward and recognition systems need to touch everyone's soul as well as their bank balance! Prêt à Manger have got into the groove with this. Why so? Well, it comes down to the Three Rs of motivation.

Recruitment

Prêt hires 'oven-ready' people with attitude and then lets them be themselves. Lou Reed rightly said, 'I do me better than anyone else', and he hasn't even got an MBA! Most companies hire people for their knowledge and skills and sack them for their attitude. Prêt's simple reversal has dramatic effects. Three-quarters of managers are promoted internally and the rest are hired with relevant work experience. Staff get an input on who joins their team.

Rewards

Staff are eligible for bonuses from Day One. They also get generous awards if they get commendations from customers and mystery shoppers. Pay rates are better than average in the sector.

Recognition

Prêt throws a party for all staff every six months and has Friday-night drinks once a month. As a routine, staff are not subject to ritual humiliation by having to wear ridiculous uniforms, clean toilets or dress up as a mascot, and so on.

Stairway to creativity?

Creativity is intimately involved with reaching self-actualisation, nirvana or whatever you want to call what you truly desire. Let's pull the plug on the mythology that says creativity is just about wearing funny hats in meetings, smoking dope, indulging in mystical business activities and so on. Instead, let's look at how creativity actually works when you are on a natural high. Extreme dissatisfaction and extreme optimism both have the power to fuel creative thinking. For example, James Dyson was both fed up with a vacuum cleaner that did not suck and had the positive disposition and technical expertise to do something about it. He spent a great deal of time getting his bagless cleaner to work, and then conducted a highly successful challenge to existing market players. So look at both ends of the spectrum, summed up in the phrase 'not only but also', to quote the comic genius Peter Cook. Here are a few.

Not only solitude but also teamwork

In a study of managers by Roffey Park, a well-known management institute, more than 60 per cent said that they found solitude helped gain access to ideas. In some cases solitude meant simply a quiet place to reflect and think. This explains why brainstorming sessions do not always work for the more inner-directed people in a team. Most of us do not have the luxury of an isolation chamber in the office to deal with the need to 'wander lonely as a cloud'. However, it is possible to achieve relative solitude in corporate life. This validates the real purpose of corridors, cubicles, smoking areas, lifts and toilets at work. Even better if the management provides custom places for this activity. We return to this on page 140 with the Pfizer example.

There is also much evidence that people are stimulated into thinking creative thoughts by interacting with others. This works best for those people who need to externalise their ideas in order to understand or appreciate them. Have you ever taken a group of people round your business to explain what it does and suddenly found yourself having a completely new appreciation of how all the different parts work together? For these types of people, team-based creativity approaches work well.

Rock'n'Roll creativity

'Any problem in the world can be solved by dancing.'

James Brown

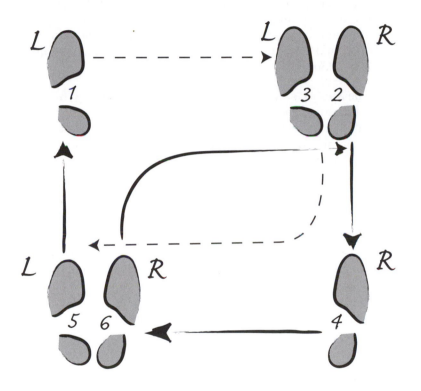

Brown is prone to exaggeration. For example, he also said 'sex machine', which is probably inaccurate, and 'funky chicken', which is pure fantasy.

Yet, he has something with his point on dancing. Movement helps us think. Have you ever had a good idea on the train, while driving, indulging in a sport? How can you increase your moving moments at work and play?

Not only immersion but also distraction

The history of creativity is full of examples of people discovering things when they are off-task or distracted — taking a shower or eating their cornflakes – as well as many examples that illustrate the conventional wisdom of total immersion. Off-task distractions – when you are engaged in something physically demanding, such as playing an instrument, playing sport or walking – are times when you can allow creative thoughts to pop into your mind. The trick is to welcome these interruptions and wonder, 'What is this telling me?' There are many examples of people inventing world-changing ideas when doing things such as washing up, ironing, and so on. As well as the discovery of gravity while its discoverer was sitting in the bath – or was it under a tree? (bet you wish you had done that), some other examples demonstrate the value of distraction:

- George de Mestral saw the need for Velcro after returning from a walk to discover seed pods stuck to his socks. On further examination, he saw that the pods had hooks, which had become entangled in the fibres of the wool. He then set about reproducing this biological quality in the material that came to be known as Velcro. Just check a moment. How much Velcro have you got on?

- Alastair Pilkington had the insightful moment that led to the perfection of float glass while he was washing the dishes. Had he just been inspired at this point, nothing further would have come of it. The really bright things that Pilkington did after this involved a shift from inspiration to perspiration: he physically tried the idea out and having found out how to do it he then went on to patent it. His idea involved building a washing-up bowl the size of a football pitch, filling it with molten tin and floating glass on top of it. Not something you can do in your lunchtime!

How can you use distraction to advantage? If your work culture does not allow you to sit in baths or do the washing-up while at work, how can you disguise some of these more outlandish approaches so that they look acceptable?

Creativity does not always mean throwing money at the problem

At the height of the space race in the 1960s, NASA commissioned the development of a ballpoint pen capable of writing under zero-gravity conditions. The Astronaut Pen was finally developed at a cost of about $1 million. The pen worked and also enjoyed some success as a novelty item.

The Soviet Union, faced with the same problem, used a pencil.

Which projects is your business overengineering?

Not only expertise but also naïveté

Sometimes expert views are essential. Other times a completely naïve view helps. Here are some examples of naïveté as a stimulus to creativity:

■ Bette Nesmith Graham was a secretary who discovered a way of covering up mistakes by observing how signwriters did this. She then scaled the process down using water-based paint and a small brush. After five years of working with her son's chemistry teacher, she perfected the formula for liquid paper.

■ Alexander Graham Bell was inspired to develop the telephone when he read an account, written in German, describing an invention that he thought would work as a telephone. After demonstrating his first working telephone, Bell discovered that he had misunderstood the report because of the language barrier, and that the German invention had an entirely different function. What a great cock-up! Think about some of the great disasters in your business that turned around and became hits. What does this say about your own creativity and self-actualisation?

■ Do you prefer isolation to working with others to gain access to creativity? If so, make reflective space in your days at work. Or you could buy yourself one of those saline isolation tanks for the office!

■ Can you systematically introduce creative stimuli into your work pattern? Go for a walk in the park or out in the country to see things differently. Does listening to music distract you, or does it bring a different focus?

■ If you are a subject expert, can you feign naïveté, at least for a while? If it feels embarrassing, make sure people know it's an act by telling them that you have temporarily regressed, or blame a rock star by saying, 'This is what Jimi Hendrix would have said.'

How do we encourage others to get a natural high? We lead them. That's next.

Natural highs

Hire experts *and* idiots if you want more creativity.

Feign stupidity by pretending to be a rock star. You're guaranteed not to be blamed for saying stupid things if you tell them that Elton John, the Bee Gees or some other rock star said it! In any case, the sublime often comes out of the ridiculous if you look hard enough.

Leadership, a.k.a. drugging others

We need leadership more than management in the current age, because business is now complex and chaotic, change is continuous, and we need to reinvent ourselves every few years. People have agonised about the terms 'management' and 'leadership' over the ages. At the Academy of Rock, the definitions are clearer.

Manager: Gets gigs, organises details, introduces predictability into the band's life, for example ensuring they get to the venue. In the classic spoof rockumentary *This is Spinal Tap* the guitarist, Nigel Tuffnell, indicates that it's the band's job to be more confused than the manager, after a debacle over the design of a stage set for 'Stonehenge'. You will learn a great deal about how not to run your business from this movie. Simply reverse the lessons and you have a management learning experience! *This is Spinal Tap* is recommended viewing as the sensible alternative to a week-long business school seminar.

Leader: Pulls the band together in terms of style and direction, inspires the audience etc. Attend a stadium gig to observe the way in which good rock stars lead their audience through an emotional roller coaster. Just think how Marc Bolan, Jim Morrison, Nirvana, Madonna and Prince do this (a bit hard to go and see Bolan, Morrison and Kurt Cobain of Nirvana these days, of course). In the rock world, the crowd-control techniques used by rock stars are the same ones used to whip up revolutions and world wars in our recent history. That does not demean their value, but does point out the need for leaders in all walks of life to question their own motives and value systems.

Leadership unplugged

Management is doing things right.

Leadership is doing the right things.

Both are needed.

Mixing music and leadership

The leader's job is to:

▪ Create sufficient explicit and implicit **structure** to mobilise people to action rather than letting chaos rule. In music this is the equivalent to writing down and understanding the score. Orchestral music consists of written instructions. In rock they are more often 'understood' (possibly because some musicians I know will not do joined-up writing). In business, this means providing sufficient clarity about the destination and sufficient ambiguity about the journey for those being led.

▪ Encourage **improvisation** within the acceptable range of the corporate culture and enterprise goals. How many guitar solos will you let staff take before insisting they come back to the verse?

▪ Manage the **customer context**. This includes setting a climate for getting things done and adopting a range of leadership styles consistent with the needs of the moment and the longer-term.

▪ Integrate all three of the above elements (structure, improvisation and customer context) into a harmonious whole, symbolised in the diagram by the place in which all three systems meet.

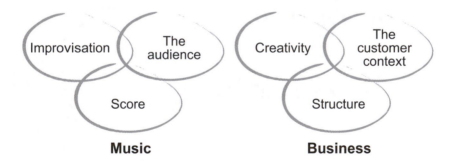

All models simplify reality. In this case, leading a company is more complicated than leading a band (unless it's Spinal Tap). However, leadership is partly the art of making the complex compellingly simple. There are some important lessons we can learn about focus, commitment, direction and flexibility from this area. Let's first look at the unknown …

Hooked?

**Creative leaders encourage followers, not 'fans'.
Fans will follow you over a cliff. Followers will tell you
before it's too late!**

The Great Unknown

Page left intentionally blank

Systematic uncertainty

'D o n ' t
know what I want but I
know how to get it.' 'Don't know what
I want but I know how to get it.' 'Don't know
what I want but I know how to get it.' 'Don't know
what I want but I know how to get it.' 'Don't know what
I want but I know how to get it.' 'Don't know what I want
but I know how to get it.' 'Don't know what I want but I know
how to get it.' 'Don't know   what I want but I know how
to get it.' 'Don't know   what I want but I know
how to get it.' 'Don't   know what I want but
I know how to get it.'   'Don't know what I want
but I know how to get   it.' 'Don't know what I
want but I know how   to get it.' 'Don't know
      what I want but I know
      how to get it.' 'Don't know
      what I want but I know
      how to get it.' 'Don't know
      what I want but I know how
      to get it.' 'Don't know what
I want but I know how to
get it.' 'Don't know what
I want but I know how
to get it.' 'Don't know
what I want but I know
how to get it.' 'Don't
know what I want but
I know how to get it.'

'Don't know what I want
but I know how to get it.'
'Don't know what I want
but I know how to get it.'
'Don't know what I want
but I know how to get it.'
'Don't know what I want
but I know how to get it.'
'Don't know what I want
but I know how to get it.'

109

Systematic uncertainty

I defined leadership as 'drugging others'. One aspect of this addresses the unknown and how people respond to it. This leads us to another definition of leadership.

Leaders make and engage others with strategic decisions under conditions of high uncertainty of means, high uncertainty of ends or both means and ends.

In other words, leaders help others to deal with 'unknowingness' by helping them to make sense of complexity and chaos through metaphors, stories and interventions that reduce potential fear of the unknown.

Can we have a systematic approach to uncertainty? Crudely speaking, the answer is definitely maybe. Business uncertainty broadly divides into four boxes:

Taking these boxes one by one, leaders can respond to uncertainty in the following ways:

Box 1: Both the goal and the means of achieving it are clear. Typically, all that is needed to resolve issues of this level of difficulty is knowledge and rational thinking, maths or judgement gained through experience.

Box 2: The goal is currently unclear but the business has the capabilities to achieve the goal as it becomes clearer. Therefore, the first capability required is that of creating a clear vision. The goals proposed by visionary leadership may also be somewhat imprecise in detail but offer a future that is worth achieving. Tell the followers to 'just do it'. The details will emerge as the future unfolds. If questions of unclear goals cannot be solved positively, then political games may break out. Recall the games on pages 78-81.

At some level you are calling on improvisation rather than relying solely on a score. In other words, more Rock'n'Roll Leadership than Orchestral Management.

Structured ambiguity

'Leaders make and engage others with strategic decisions under conditions of high uncertainty of means, ends or both means and ends.'

Peter Cook

Academy of Rock

Box 3: The direction is clear but current means of achieving the goal are suboptimal. This calls for either radical or incremental creative problem solving. This requires a more systematic process than is needed for Box 2 issues. Essentially you come back to orchestral or A–Z thinking, using a structured process (score) for systematically redefining problems, generating novel and appropriate solutions, and implementing those solutions in reality.

Box 4: Neither the goal nor the means of achieving it is clear. These kinds of problems are sometimes termed 'the swamp'. At the extreme, chaos leads to bewilderment as the issue becomes increasingly complex.

For example, famine and global warming are swamplike problems, in so far as the goals are not shared by all and there are many vested interests and varying points of view, and the proposed solutions are often simplistic, which means that there are no clear winners.

We can summarise the typical responses as follows:

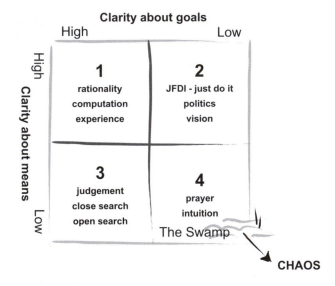

Although the matrix points up some pretty obvious things, I'm constantly surprised at how some companies apply the wrong tool for the job. For example, lengthy brainstorming sessions (Box 2) are used to solve Box 1 problems such as 'How do we compare with competitors?' when a little bit of benchmarking or the use of a knowledge-management expert would do. Box 1 solutions such as maths are often used by politicians to persuade the public that they are in command of complex Box 4 problems such as 'world peace' or 'entry to the euro monetary system'.

Orchestral Manoeuvres in The Darkness

… or how structure (scores) and creativity (improvisation) help to address uncertain problems of a strategic nature.

Broadly speaking, the A–Z, systematic, creative problem-solving approach equates to having a score for solving problems. In essence, this equates to the idea of orchestral management.

In contrast, the Z–A approach to visioning the future is more about using improvisation. In essence, this equates to the idea of Rock'n'Roll Leadership.

But the matrix does flag up roughly where on the radar screen you are. This helps leaders eliminate the wrong approaches and focuses debate where the problem is, depending on uncertainty levels. This can be a considerable help. The leader's job then is to deploy the right tools for the job, for example the A–Z orchestral management approach using a systematic score, the Z–A improvisational leadership approach.

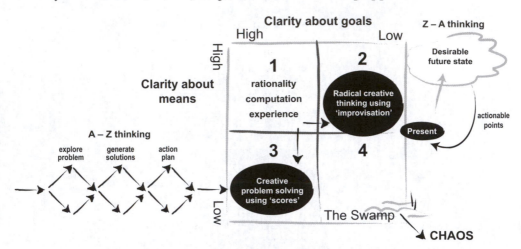

We've used the processes that go with this approach to clarify strategic direction and come up with innovative products and services for drug and telecoms companies – see the story opposite. In both cases, this crude analysis saves immense amounts of time and helps people understand the true nature of what they are trying to deal with.

Creative Leadership is about applying strategies that systematically reduce the area of Box 4, a.k.a. 'the swamp':

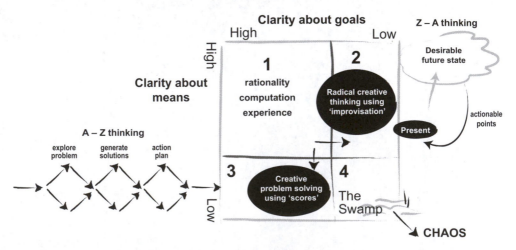

This town ain't big enough for the both of us: Z–A and A–Z thinking in action

This example from our own consultancy portfolio illustrates the types of approach that can be used to deal with strategic problems of high uncertainty.

The client was a multinational drug company that was concerned about possible competition changes due to merger and acquisition. These changes threatened to erode its position in a key product area. In short, it wanted to 'head the competition off before they reached the pass'.

We designed a scenario-building exercise (Z–A thinking) and a creative-thinking exercise (A–Z thinking) to help the executive team unravel the complexity. This delivered the following benefits:

- the rehearsal of a number of possible futures (scenarios) before they happened so that they could decide which strategies to pursue; and

- the identification of early-warning signals so that the company could sense and respond rapidly to changes before they damaged their market position.

Field sales staff were alerted to the early-warning signals. When these subsequently appeared, the company was able to take preventative marketing actions some twelve months before the competitor activity would have been picked up conventionally. This meant that it was able to stay ahead of the game. This strategy had an impact on bottom-line results that could be measured in millions.

The company also initiated a proactive research-and-development strategy to allow it to sustain its position in the market. This meant that, as well as protecting itself in the short-term, it was able to build a long-term position.

The process reduced the size of the swamp by making the unknown increasingly known, so that the company was able to take decisive strategic action in both the short- and long term.

Typical topics that crop up in each box include:

Box 1: Where shall we source paperclips from? What is the rate of VAT? Solutions include: for paperclips apply judgement or look in the office-supplies catalogue; for VAT rates ask an expert or look the answer up on the website. You do not need a three-day creative problem-solving meeting to put out a national tender for suppliers of paperclips or to discuss the VAT rate. Sadly, though, this sort of thing happens!

Box 2: Where should we be targeting our effort or leveraging our core competences in the next five to ten years? Approaches such as strategic visioning, projective methods, where art or music can be used to articulate fuzzy futures and scenario modelling are helpful here.

Box 3: Can we improve our current products and services to keep us ahead of the competition? Creative problem-solving tools such as brainstorming, reverse brainstorming, superheroes and creativity checklists are useful here and have been applied in cases such as a pharmaceutical company wishing to maintain and grow its market share in a specific therapy area.

Box 4: How can we act globally and locally? How can we solve violent-crime issues? At a personal level the old Clash song 'Should I Stay or Should I Go?' – in other words, changing your job or career – is often one of the most swamplike of problems. Tossing a coin, using visioning and systematic creative problem solving (Boxes 2 and 3 thinking combined) and using hunch, lunch and basic instinct are examples of a range of methods that can assist. A poor solution is to simply allow these problems to be put into the company's 'too difficult' in-tray.

If leadership is about mobilising people to perform under conditions of uncertainty, what can we say about leadership style? Read on.

SWAMP-DRAINING QUESTIONS FOR LEADERS

AFTER THE BEE GEES: HOW DEEP IS YOUR SWAMP?

ARE THERE ANY CROCODILES THERE?

HOW BIG ARE THEY? WHAT
DO THEY WANT?

CAN YOU ADD ANY PREDATORS?

The leader of the cats?

Leading creative people and companies has been likened to the herding of cats. In general, cats resist direction from others, have their own territories, which they jealously guard and spray, and have whims, egos etc. My own experience of leading teams of R&D scientists reinforces this view, and I spent a good deal of my early life getting scientists to follow a general direction rather than disappearing off into quiet corners (cat baskets) to pursue their own interests, scratch, lick their bums, sleep and do other cat things. In short, many creative people resist being managed but can be led.

Leadership style is one of the least understood areas of business, which is perhaps why there are so many books (and songs) on the subject. Some preach a single style and suggest that leadership is a mystical quality that can be acquired only through divine (or genetic) intervention. Others come from a more pragmatic angle and say it's merely a bag of techniques. Still others suggest it's about behavioural flexibility. It's all of these and more. Unless you are running a one-person business with a single product and a single customer whose needs do not change from one year to the next, then you will need to be flexible – but without trying to be all things to all people.

That's fine as far as it goes. Most of us have a range of styles that we are comfortable with and others that we revert to under pressure. In rock music this means playing the old hits – it constantly surprises me how people still enjoy playing 'Alright Now' by Free and 'Black Magic Woman' by Santana at a jam session. I confess that even I have played these numbers on occasion. In business, this means reverting to type. In other words, using the style you are most comfortable with even if it does not fit the circumstances. The range of leadership styles may be depicted as follows:

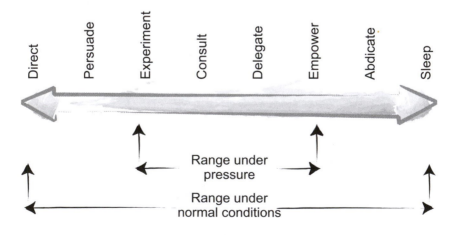

My way?

Frank Sinatra may have misled a generation of leaders who used his approach to inform their leadership style with his song 'My Way'. One way to look at Frank's song is where 'My Way' means 'flair'. This is OK. However, the dark side of 'My Way' offers leaders the excuse of not listening, being dogmatic, bull-headed, slavishly following best practice recipes rather than thinking for ourselves etc.

Had Frank sung the lyric 'I did it their way' the song would probably not have been a hit. After all, nobody likes a pop singer or a leader who doesn't know their own mind! However, he would have refocused our attention on some of the features of modern leaders:

1. The leader juggles a number of competing influences in a given situation and comes up with a style that best fits the situation. You may have noticed that these words do not scan into 'My Way' very well – never mind! Key questions that leaders must ask include:

    Needs: What leadership style does this situation need of me right now while I'm still keeping an eye on the future?

    Ability/Motivation: Am I able and willing to operate in this style?

    Morals and ethics: Is it right that I adopt this strategy and behaviour in terms of the stakeholders that will be affected by my approach?

    Consequences: What are the consequences, now and into the future?

2. The leader listens to his/her stakeholders but retains the right to make unpopular decisions. This is different from 'death by consultation', whereby leaders fail to decide or make decisions that are the lowest common denominator of everybody's opinions.

3. The leader manages the expectations of those positively and adversely affected by change. This increasingly includes more than just the immediate set of stakeholders. 'Drugging shareholders' when the news is bad now comes down to the quality of the food and drink available at the annual shareholder meeting!

Top Cat – 'My Way' in practice

William Steere, former CEO of Pfizer, offers six lessons for leaders:

1. Focus on what you do best.

2. Cast a wide net – look inside and outside.

3. Create transparent objectives.

4. Listen to divergent points of view.

5. Create a culture of trust.

6. Go with your instincts.

From the ballroom floor to the boardroom floor?

A while back I met an entrepreneur who developed a novel bra-manufacturing business for large-breasted women. We were talking about what drove her to form the business. She cited abject poverty, some serious family impediments, a desire to be different. She also mentioned that her approach to her business and personal life was more informed by the song 'I Will Survive' as performed by Gloria Gaynor, rather than anything she learned formally. Just as well she chose this song rather than 'We Hate It When Our Friends Become Successful' by Morrissey or a Lou Reed or Leonard Cohen number! This demonstrates just how powerful such acquired anchors can be in directing our beliefs and behaviours. In her case, the song was a much stronger driver of her performance than anything she might have learned at business school. Some academics might be concerned about this. Others might be making the connection that it's not the business school's academic curriculum that really matters, but what records the DJ plays at the end-of-term disco. What are the songs that motivate you, pick you up when you're down, act as a rallying call or as a challenge to 'enemies'?

I'm not claiming that music can change your strategic viewpoint or core competences. But you may have noticed just how many songs are about leadership in one form or another. Even more interesting is the fact that the titles shine a light on the different facets of this genuinely complex and mystical topic. What other songs have messages in them for leaders? Enter the Rock'n'Roll Leadership Academy opposite.

Next we'll look at the different types of people a creative leader must lead. This is especially relevant if your business must innovate in its brand, products/services or internal processes.

Rock'n'Roll Leadership Academy

Academy of Rock	Business School Translation
Bridge over troubled water	Team coach, counsellor, mediator, resource in difficult times.
Respect	Someone who gives respect to all levels of people and who gains it in return.
If you love someone, set them free	'The boss empowers me to do things I didn't know I could do – although they are always there if I need them, they don't appear to watch over me.'
Try a little tenderness	Someone who gets things done easily – they could probably get tough, but never need to.
The king of wishful thinking	A born optimist – nothing seems to bother them. However, they need to be surrounded by pragmatists to ensure their ideas can be executed.
Stand by me	'I know that I will be supported by this person if I make a mistake – it's like having a safety net if you are walking the high wire.'
Billy, don't be a hero	Leadership is not about the lone heroic personality. It's much more about a team approach and engaging others. At least that's my reading of the song. Opinions vary!

These descriptions illustrate that there is no single standard of leadership. What works in one situation may be largely inappropriate in another. Over time, what people require from a leader also changes. This explains why some leaders have a limited shelf life. Smart leaders develop mechanisms for sensing the ever-changing moods of their followers and adjust their style to respect these needs over time.

A chain reaction – Creative Leadership

It's one thing leading people. It's quite another leading people involved in innovative product or service development. At least four roles are crucial in ensuring the successful conversion of an idea to a successful innovation. Enter the 'chain reaction for innovation':

$$I + I + C + E = IP$$

Inventor + Innovator + Champion + Entrepreneur
=
Innovation Potential

Creative Leadership therefore responds to the differing needs and styles of these roles in an innovation process. Taking each role in turn:

The **Inventor** is the person who generates the idea in its initial form.

Inventors are often single-minded people who are addicted to their field of interest. At the extreme these people are so hooked on their invention that they fail to do the sex (relationship) stuff. However, there are notable exceptions: inventors such as Thomas Edison and more recently James Dyson who possess the relationship and business skills needed to take an idea to the marketplace. More often, these qualities are missing. The best that inventors can do in such circumstances is to recognise this weakness and surround themselves with people with the relevant talents. Bill Gates is a good example of someone who has done this in the business world. In the rock business, we will study punk icon John Otway as an example of an all-rounder in the Rock'n'Roll chapter. John is singer, songwriter, performer and marketer – unlike Beethoven, who stuck to inventing and left others to interpret, perform and promote his works.

Inventors are often thought of as impossible people to manage, although they may still be led, given the appropriate motivation. As well as being impossible, they are motivated by the thought of doing impossible things. They display characteristics such as persistence, curiosity, boundless energy, risk taking and the ability to figure things out. Leaders need to find ways to create work and projects that give inventors these outcomes, while maintaining a sense of direction. Tricky but not impossible.

ADDICTED TO LOVE

In 1933, Harry Beck invented the groundbreaking design for the London Tube map. He was still improving his design decades later, in spite of the fact that London Underground had paid him only five guineas. After his death he did get a plaque on the wall of Finchley Central Station acknowledging all his hard work.

The **Innovator** is the person responsible for realising the idea.

Innovators develop the final product or service in a form that the market will accept. In modern companies, this may be a team rather than a single person. Innovators are skilled problem solvers, knocking down barriers to innovation along the way, may be more realistic than the inventors, often require a degree of autonomy and like to use their initiative. They need support, encouragement and resources from a leader.

The **Champion** is that influential person who secures resources for the idea and defends it against critics.

Champions are usually skilled networkers who will move an idea around the enterprise or outside through their extensive network of contacts. More importantly they will defend it from attack at the early stages when the idea is essentially unproven and therefore defenceless from corporate attack.

Champions have qualities such as the ability and willpower to stand against the status quo, have a wide social network extending across the whole enterprise to the world outside, and will be perceived as a trusted broker of new ideas, having independence of thought rather than blind faith. They will mobilise support for an idea, help convert features into benefits and have the interpersonal skills and savvy to get under the skin of the enterprise's political defences. Leaders must respond to these needs and characteristics.

The **Entrepreneur** is the person who takes on financial risks or persuades others to do so in order to bring the innovation to market.

Entrepreneurs know how to spend their own and other people's money. They are skilled dealmakers and persuaders. They can package an idea or an invention into a business case and present this to others so that it attracts resources. Key qualities of entrepreneurs include drive, opportunism and risk taking, and show little respect for authority.

Leaders may gain favour by legitimising the more irritating parts of the entrepreneur's style.

Great innovations of our time

1900 The paper clip

1914 The bra

1918 Frigidaire refrigerator

1921 RCA radio

1935 Kodachrome film

1954 Fender Stratocaster

1959 Xerox photocopier

1971 Intel microcomputer

1982 Philips/Sony CD

1991 World Wide Web

The innovation formula in action

I + I + C + E = IP

Inventor + Innovator + Champion + Entrepreneur
=
Innovation Potential

The example of the photocopier illustrates the innovation formula. Chester Carlson invented xerography out of his frustration with existing methods of copying documents. He found innovative support and a champion in the form of the Battelle Institute in Germany and the Haloid Corporation (later to be named Xerox) provided the entrepreneurship to bring the product to market. The photocopier probably revolutionised work in the latter half of the 20th century, while simultaneously allowing us to overload ourselves with information. Despite the more unusual uses that the photocopier has been put to, such as copying various parts of office anatomy, I'd judge it to be one of the more useful innovations of our time.

Innovation in most modern companies is complex. It usually needs all the roles whether in one person or a team. But the formula is not a recipe. For example, the vacuum cleaner was originally conceived by a department store cleaner who had asthma and wanted to stop creating dust when using his broom. The inventor did not see the wider applications of his invention and it took his brother-in-law (William Hoover) to see the potential – and proceed to make it famous. Hoover was also good at marketing, inventing appealing hooks such as 'It beats as it sweeps as it cleans'. He could have been a rock star with lyrics like that! Eventually the Hoover Corporation developed corporate myopia and was then surprised by the invention of Dyson's bagless vacuum cleaner (see page 98).

Key point

If you lead innovative projects, do you have all the talents necessary to ensure you have the best chance of success?

How can you vary your style to deal with inventor types at the same time as entrepreneurs? Can you get them to work together in harmony?

The gurus of leadership authenticity

'You go to leadership school, and try to pitch your voice the same way that the boss did there, and have your office decorated the same way his is, and that's not real leadership. Real leadership probably has more to do with recognising your own uniqueness than it does with identifying your similarities.'

Sydney Pollack

'I do me better than anyone else.'

Lou Reed

Summary

Motivation is about finding which business drugs work for you. Inner- or outer-directed? Motivated by must dos or might dos? No need for ecstasy or herbal remedies!

The Three Fs of Leadership are about Finding, Feeling and Feeding the natural highs and addictions that make people come to work and keep on coming.

Many HR systems do not motivate – they simply place obstacles between those that do the work and those who wish to engage them. Some companies have recognised this and have set up simple but meaningful ways of hooking their staff.

Feeling comfortable with not knowing the answer is a hallmark of successful leadership. This is different from being dumb.

Creative leaders create circumstances where people can ask frightening questions and take calculated risks. This ensures that the business keeps its eyes and ears open to disruptive changes.

Different leadership styles are needed to encourage innovation. We noted the formula of inventors, innovators, champions and entrepreneurs. Each of these roles demands a different leadership style. More a case of 'I did it their way'.

Questions to ask back at the ranch

Three sets of questions to pose next time you're on stage:

1. Why do people come to work here? What aspects of work increase their sense of why they come? What would make things better? Can we remove dissatisfiers, add satisfiers or both?

2. What leadership songs are you/we singing at work, either consciously or otherwise? Are they the right ones?

3. What experiences do you put your leaders through to increase their ability to act when the destination or journey is unclear?

Dialogue 3

Rock'n'Roll

Rock on ...
High Performance

We rock, therefore we are.

Have you ever been to a really great gig? The best performers in the world come on stage as if it were already the encore and take it on up from there. Whether it's out-and-out rock acts such as AC/DC, Deep Purple, Guns N' Roses, Janis Joplin, The Darkness or the Red Hot Chili Peppers, all-round performers such as Madonna, Prince and Kylie or something more sublime, such as Kate Bush, BB King, Peter Gabriel, Nina Simone, Sinatra, Streisand or Motörhead. The point is that top acts know how to hit peak performance, time after time. How does this translate into the crazy world of work?

There's no rehearsal on stage. If something goes wrong, you gotta roll with it, unlike business, where you can call another meeting or delay the project deadlines. This means: a great deal of practice beforehand; the ability to improvise and profit from accidents along the way; or a bit of both. These are the skills of high performance, whether it's in the world of music or at work. Let there be rock! Let it roll!

High performance requires the following elements:

- **Preparation** – both mental and physical. The important thing about rehearsal is that you leave sufficient room to take advantage of surprises, pleasant or otherwise.
- **Delivery and execution** – the vision, foresight and the detailed, sequential thinking needed to ensure smooth execution.
- **Learning and reinvention** – noticing what actually happens, and then improving your current performance levels. Sometimes you must start over to keep yourself alive.

Let's start with preparation.

FOR THOSE ABOUT TO MEET, WE SALUTE YOU ...

Do you start your project management meetings as if you had reached the encore?

What would happen if you did?

Watch some AC/DC live concert footage to see what high-voltage performance is really all about.

The importance of being earnestly prepared

Seamless performance in any field comes from both hard work *and* serendipity, not either/or of these alternatives. Therefore we need to look at the spectrum between planning and creativity. I often meet people who tell me they are creative, yet this is sometimes a euphemism for being disorganised and never delivering anything. As such, they give creativity a bad name. Creativity without perspiration is about as useful as an Olympic runner reaching the finishing line but on the wrong day (due to meeting a special friend along the way and taking some time out for a meal and some networking …). In business, not only do you have to be creative – there are plenty of people with ideas out there – but you also have to innovate and successfully convert your ideas into profitable results. This requires blood, sweat and sometimes tears. It's no wonder that the great pretenders run when the word 'work' crops up in conversation.

Practice may be dull but it's vital, especially if your contribution must mesh with others'. Amateur musicians think that preparation is about drinking lots of beer and staying up late, and that practising is for sissies. The difference between amateur and professional musicians is that the pros manage to fit in what they must do to excel with the drinking and staying up late.

Practice does not always have to involve *physical* practice. Mental preparation is just as important as the physical variety. Top sports stars spend a good deal of their time preparing mentally. This includes visualising the successful moves they intend to make. Sometimes this has more impact than the physical preparation, since that tends to involve the rehearsal of failure.

What physical and mental preparation rituals do you use to achieve peak performance? How could you extend the range?

Perspiration

+

Inspiration

=

Innovation

Seamless performance comes from hard work and serendipity.

In other words, you can profit from the unexpected if you have done the preparation.

From the Academy of Rock...

Something in the air …

Some people waste a great deal of time and money trying to establish or change the corporate culture to achieve performance improvements that fade away fast. There is also an increasing tendency to establish monocultures – perhaps because it enables corporate slaves to sing the Queen song 'One Vision, One Mission' at conferences? In the real world, we need different subcultures for addressing the differing functions, the types of people and customers that they serve. In most situations, the 'One Vision, One Mission' approach is unnecessarily restrictive and only serves HR's need for tidiness. It does very little to improve performance.

One way to have your cake and eat it too is to vary the climate at work to reflect different needs at particular times. Musically, this relates to setting the stage, getting lights, smoke, groupies, roadies, sound systems etc. At work, it relates to setting up the physical and psychological environment so that people can perform at their best. Climate differs from culture in that it's about the atmosphere or mood of the business or part of it, rather than its deeply felt values and beliefs. It's easier to change the climate in response to particular needs, and it is particularly important to be able to vary the climate when you have a very strong corporate culture such as Microsoft, GlaxoSmithKline and MacDonald's.

What has this got to do with music? Well, musicians are excellent mood magicians and take their audiences through a series of different microclimates during a performance. Consider how Elvis, Madonna, Bruce Springsteen, Tina Turner et al. manage the audience's mood from ecstasy, through melancholy, reflection, regret, anger to excitement and climax. To achieve this, they vary both the content of the performance and the presentation or image. I have already noted the huge difference in energy between the dance floor and the factory floor. There is much to learn from this contrast, not just the use of smoke, strobe lights and exotic dancers in your business meetings.

Creative climate unplugged

Musicians crucially understand the impact of atmosphere on performance.

How does your business get into a high-performance groove?

In the heat of the night?

Have you ever attended a jam session? The climate is the smoke in the room, the intolerable crush of people, the smell of hot sweaty bodies joined in a collective passion for music. It's the feeling of anticipation that hangs in the air when the guitar player takes the lead without warning. It's wondering if it's going to go horribly wrong or whether you are about to witness something truly original. It's not easy to define or reproduce. When someone says 'you had to be there' they are talking climate. So let's talk about climate.

In his research on organisational climate the Swedish Professor, Göran Ekvall, studied what went on in a Swedish newspaper office. He discovered that the team working on the women's pages were always winning prizes while the newsroom never did. On further analysis, the biggest difference between the teams was in their sense of humour. Sounds like the newsroom team were singin' the blues –– and that makes sense, doesn't it, always having to report on the dark side of the moon? (More on the blues opposite.) A sense of humour does not appear as a line on the company balance sheet, but clearly this intangible asset makes a critical difference in this and many other examples.

The physical and psychological environment is a key component of a high-performance climate. Some people need quiet reflective space, others need close friends, others the comfort of strangers. Some need a means of keeping focus, others a distraction from the main point of the creative work etc. At the extreme, artists, dancers, actors, musicians and poets have lived in cold water, cut off their ears, lived in walk-up apartments, moved to the Left Bank in Paris or adopted unusual lifestyles. Yet, there's no guarantee that these approaches will work for you. What does?

Leading companies recognise the vital impact of climate on the performance and try to influence this in ways that lead to success. Sometimes this is an accident, in the sense that it's not consciously understood. On other occasions, it's designed in a well-considered way. Let's look at some examples of a designed approach after the blues interlude.

A blues climate?

Most blues begin, 'Woke up this morning …'. 'I got a good woman' is a bad way to begin the blues, unless you stick something nasty in the next line such as, 'I got a good woman, with the meanest face in town.' You can't have a blues that begins, 'I got a good manager, who sets meaningful performance goals and critical success factors.'

The blues ain't about A–Z creative problem-solving, brainstorming sessions, option formulation or scenario planning: you stuck in a ditch, you stuck in a ditch – ain't no way out.

Blues cars: Chevys, Fords, Cadillacs and broken-down trucks.

Blues don't travel in Volvos, BMWs, or sport-utility vehicles. You can have the last train to Clarksville, but not Cirencester. There are no trains to heaven as the seventies pop-art band Be-Bop Deluxe succinctly put it.

Blues can take place in New York City, but not in Rochester or any place in Canada. Hard times in Minneapolis or Canterbury are probably just clinical depression. Chicago, St Louis and Kansas City are still the best places to have the blues, not York, Bath or Slough. You cannot have the blues in any place that don't get rain.

You can't have no blues in a shopping mall. The lighting is all wrong.

Acceptable blues beverages are: cheap wine, whisky or bourbon, muddy water. The following are *not* blues beverages: Perrier, Chardonnay, Pimm's or Slim Fast.

If death occurs in a cheap motel or a shotgun shack, it's a blues death. Stabbed in the back by a jealous lover is another blues way to die. So are the electric chair and substance abuse. You can't have a blues death if you expire during a strategy meeting, a team-building day, on an overnight stay at the Holiday Inn, or while receiving liposuction.

People with names like Michelle, Amber, Jade, Debbie and Heather can't sing the blues, no matter how many men they shoot in the 'twin blues towns' of Memphis, Milton Keynes or Milan.

Atom shop – Stimulating the climate at Pfizer

Pfizer regards innovation as central to its long-term future in bringing new drugs to market. It also recognises the importance of the built environment in creating a climate where innovation is more probable and frequent. It has modelled this into the design of its research-and-development facility in the UK. The entrance to its laboratories is via a number of atria, where employees can:

- spend time alone, reflecting on issues that concern or interest them;
- interact with other people, of similar professions or different ones;
- indulge in on-task learning and play; and
- indulge in off-task learning and play.

The different atria offer a variety of ways of learning. Mixing across the campus is also encouraged – allowing for improvisation without overt orchestration.

A climate for collaboration

Arthur Anderson's London office has taken the physical aspects of climate seriously, by adhering to a number of environmental design principles:

- colour: a red meeting room creates energy and stimulates creativity;
- domesticity: informal furniture contrasts with formality and provides a more homely climate for those who prefer this to clean corporate modernity;
- metal: a simple café with metal tables for brief encounters of a functional nature; and
- mobility: a teamwork area called 'chaos' has mobile furniture so that groups can form rapidly to suit the needs of the moment.

The built environment is part of climate, and it affects how people behave. However, a pleasant work environment is insufficient to guarantee high performance – which brings us back to Herzberg's message about dissatisfiers.

Style Council – Smoke signals of a bad climate

We once did some work for a local government organisation that asked that we remove exclamation marks from our presentation materials.

When we enquired as to the reason, we were told that exclamation marks were 'not part of the corporate culture'.

In hindsight, we should have left straightaway or employed a gangster rapper to teach them some language!

Delivery

It's one thing to be creative, quite another to be able to execute your ideas or business strategy. Paradoxically, the skills you need for the first area are rarely accompanied by the skills needed for the second. An example of a rock star who has successfully combined both is that of English eccentric punk icon John Otway, who has survived for nearly thirty years in the UK music business in an industry where longevity is more usually measured in weeks. Inventor, innovator, champion and entrepreneur all in one! What's special about this man?

To the casual eye, John Otway is one of those 'creative musicians'. Some superficial facts about his life tend to reinforce this view:

■ Otway received the equivalent of a £1 million advance in 1977 – ten times the sum that power pop trio The Jam got. He managed to spend it all within nine months. His second hit was a flop and he went on to achieve an unbroken record of 25 flops. In this sense John is living proof of Miles Davis's maxim: 'Do not fear mistakes. There are none.' John has taken this view to its natural end!

■ He wrote a book called *Cor Baby, That's Really ME!*, which focused on his career as 'Rock'n'Roll's greatest failure', using self-effacing humour and perverse wit as a vehicle of self-instruction. He was widely told that this would be a disastrous marketing move, but proved these people wrong, basing his decision on an attitude of self-confidence.

■ Otway first spotted fame when he was nine years old, realising that he could get an audience of a hundred people to come and see him in the school playground at lunchtime by drinking a bottle of ink. One of the early hallmarks of an entrepreneur?

These facts hide the fact that Otway has carved out a career in a niche that few others are prepared to enter, i.e. the rich vein of mistakes, failures and cock-ups. Just note how few corporate seminars have these words in the title! In doing so, it becomes apparent that John is actually no fool and possesses meticulous delivery and execution skills. These are just as relevant to business as they are to Rock'n'Roll. Let's look at some of the less sensational but more important parts of Otway's skillset.

Rock tips for high performance

Get hair – in business this is called 'grooming'.

Build a massive wall in Berlin, à la Pink Floyd.

Float a statue of yourself down the River Thames à la Michael Jackson – but leave the other stuff out.

Throw TVs out of hotel room windows.

Rename your company using a postmodernist symbol and put the word SLAVE on staff uniforms.

Burn guitars after making love with them.

Put 'King Arthur on ice', as Rick Wakeman did.

Begin with the end in mind

Otway had always wanted to have a second hit, having become a one-hit wonder in 1977 with his punk rock cult classic 'Cor Baby, That's Really Free'. When his fans asked him what he wanted as a fiftieth-birthday present, he said, 'Another hit.' However, when you are fifty, you just do not get into the music charts unless you do something very different from the usual suspects. Also, the 'monopoly' music shops, such as Woolworth's, who effectively control the UK music charts, do not want their strategies for predicting what records they need to stock interfered with. So it takes extreme creativity and excellent execution skills to crack the corporate defence system. Otway set an extremely ambitious goal in so far as he booked the London Palladium one year away from his second hit so that he would have to do whatever it took to have a hit – or face public ridicule and a massive debt. This is both structure and improvisation, and from a small business entrepreneur is a calculated risk! This is real Rock'n'Roll Leadership!

Do the hard work

Otway has boundless creativity and energy. Faced with the fact that he had insufficient committed fans for getting his hit into the charts, he came up with the idea of inviting the fans to Abbey Road Studios, home of The Beatles, to perform on the B-side. Nine hundred fans came and performed with John on 'House of the Rising Sun'. Otway had figured out that if he put their names on the record as backing singers, 'not only would they buy a copy for themselves, but they would buy one for their mum', thus doubling the sales potential. This single strategy also multiplied his sales force by a factor of nine hundred at minimal cost.

How much would your business benefit if it could multiply its unpaid sales force or client relationship team nine hundred times?

If your business has to operate within a monopoly with a dominant player, what transferable learning points can you take from Otway's Punk Rock Marketing Strategy (coming up in two pages' time) to crack the corporate defence system?

Give it head-butts – Lessons in delivery and execution from John Otway

Begin with the end in mind.

Do the hard work.

Deal with details as well as the big picture.

If what you are doing isn't working do something different rather than bash your head against the same wall.

Find cracks in the system that nobody else has spotted.

Enjoy what you do – relish every performance as if it were the first time.

All the small things make a big difference

Little things can make the difference between success and failure. Often, things fail because there are too many strategists and not enough executioners. Here are some of the little things John did.

He ensured that he kept his fans briefed with intelligence on how the hit campaign was proceeding, and let them use their initiative rather than trying to control everything. For example, the norm for record sales in the UK is for only 40 per cent of the stock to be sold. This figure is so low because the other 60 per cent of the stock is in the wrong places where people cannot buy it. Otway increased his sales to 70 per cent of the total stock in the market by encouraging fans to email one another about where in the country stock was lying unsold. They would then clear those shops where stock was available.

How can you supply your customers with information that helps them to help you? How can you find cracks in the system?

He gained access to all the main TV channels and the press. Woolworth's refused to stock the record because they claimed their market was young girls and that nobody wanted to see John in the charts. Channel 4 News took up the story using the angle of 'small man crushed by corporate giant'. This significantly helped sell more records and resulted in the dismissal of their director for public relations in a classic PR goof. Woolworth's foolishly defended their position, instead of saying that 'the whole thing was a great stunt and we are fully behind John, having been taken by surprise by his success'. They could have then profited from maintaining a good public image.

What can you learn from this PR mistake?

He hung in there. Eventually the strategy paid off. The London Palladium was full and the single hit the charts at Number 9. His next project is a world tour, taking in the Carnegie Hall, Caesar's Palace, Sydney Opera House, Geneva Convention Rooms and the Royal Albert Hall. What can you learn about setting extremely audacious goals and not giving up when the odds are against you?

John Otway's website can be found at www.johnotway.com. Human Dynamics also arrange corporate conferences and events with John, combining substantial educational/business content with pure enjoyment/entertainment. Serious fun: a powerful mixture!

We next turn our attention to the issue of experimentation and improvisation. At the extreme, we are talking about being able to respond under conditions of complexity and chaos. Let it roll …

Delivery problems unplugged

Too many strategists and not enough executioners.
Too many executioners and no strategy.

Chaos and disorder

Why did the stock market crash more than five hundred points one day in 1987?

Why do weather forecasters frequently get predictions drastically wrong? For example, weathermen have told us 'It's raining cats and dogs' and The Weather Girls did once tell us 'It's Raining Men'.

Would the business world be better if it were more predictable?

Is the purchase of stocks in ice cream and umbrellas the best way to secure a balanced portfolio of risks, or can we trust people who produce graphs about the future?

We now know that we are not in control of the world around us and that small events are joined up in a complex system. Try getting a champion fund manager to repeat their performance in Years 2 and 3! We have already visited the state of chaos on pages 112-7 as a place beyond 'the swamp'. As we understand more how dynamic systems work, it is vital to understand how chaos theory can be applied to business.

Chaos refers not just to the unknown, but to the unknowable. In other words, chaos is a form of instability where the specific details of the long-term future are unknowable. Chaos is about irregular patterns of behaviour that may be driven by external events, some of which may be far removed from the present context and therefore 'invisible' to most observers. Success in business therefore arises from responding appropriately to a number of interrelated amplifying effects that cannot be predicted in advance. In such a world people and businesses need to be not only nimble but also thoughtful.

Most chaos theorists have been preoccupied by the notion that order emerges from chaos through processes of spontaneous self-organisation. The more surprising insight is to notice that chaos can emerge from order. A certain amount of order or structure in business can be good for 'useful chaos'. That's fine in theory, but what does it mean in practice for leaders? Enter the Chaos Disciplines …

The chaos guru

Management guru Ralph Stacey provided us with the insight that structure emerges from chaos through positive and negative feedback. The more surprising insight is that chaos can emerge from excessive structure. Some governments have known this for many years!

The chaos disciplines

To respond to chaos, leaders must:

1. Gain control by letting go and developing more trust in the ability of the system or group of people to self-organise. This is where orchestra conductors throw away the sheet music and baton and where the jamming begins.

2. Use power elegantly. Elegance is a vital part of getting the results you really desire. This means using the minimum type, level and polarity of power necessary to achieve results and the means of getting them, rather than relying on submission or encouraging rebellion in order to reach your goals. Power type, level and polarity are defined as:

■ **Types of power** – You get power from your *position* or from your ability to control *resources*, human, financial and technical. These forms of power are mostly given to you. Power also comes in forms that must be earned: *social* (networking) power; *expertise* in a discipline; *personal* power or charisma; and the power that comes from having and using *information*.

■ **Level** refers to the degree of leverage necessary and whether power is used overtly or covertly.

■ **Polarity** refers to how power is used positively or negatively. We looked at negative uses of power in the form of some of the political games people play under 'Dialogue 1: Sex' (see pages 78-81).

All this adds up to a completely different and more socially responsible use of power. It also needs what Prince would call a new kind of 'New Power Generation' to cope with this responsibility. Are you ready for this?

What business gurus say about chaos as a paradox

We are fundamentally pulled in two directions, one expanding and the other converging. How can we profit from this paradox by synthesising contradictions rather than fighting for an either/or resolution?

What the Academy of Rock says about the paradox

You gotta roll with it …

So a useful question becomes:

How can I meet the need for novelty, while at the same time building a firm foundation for my business?

Become more comfortable with paradoxes and try to synthesise apparent opposites using *and/also*, rather than trying to make *either/or* judgements. For example: How do we reward individuals and teams? How do we retain customers by setting them free? and so on.

3. Try to *resolve* complex problems rather than solve them. A tactical solution to a swamplike problem, which is inherently complex and ambiguous and has many different viewpoints, often makes the problem worse in the whole system. A good example of a swamplike problem would be 'fixing transport in London, Mumbai or Bangkok'.

4. Tolerate subcultures and conflict over ideas rather than insisting on a slavish adherence to a mission. Hire argumentative people.

5. Present ambiguous challenges rather than sticking to specific objectives and other convergent approaches to management.

6. Encourage staff to challenge organisational practices, myths and views from above, for example by the implementation of a well-thought-out suggestions scheme.

7. Allow the business to face risky environments that put its innovation talents to the test in order to stay ahead of the game.

8. Develop people's skills in what business guru Peter Senge calls systems thinking, so they can recognise vicious and virtuous circles, see both the wood and the trees and devise elegant interventions at critical break points.

9. Value intuition at least as strongly as analytical thinking, possibly more so in cultures that are biased in favour of analysis over feel. Be cautious about the trap of relying solely on gut feeling, as with the Cornflake Girl story earlier. Back up your intuitions with reasoned argument.

10. Replace forecasts with dress rehearsals for alternative future scenarios. (Dresses may be worn if required, but are not essential to success.) At a grand level, dress rehearsals can be formalised as scenario planning. At a personal level this involves a great deal of mental what-iffing.

Symbols, signs and sex

Love him or hate him, the musician Prince is a master of improvisation, and many of his performances are loosely coupled jams. Yet, to achieve this seamless level of performance, Prince uses significant elements of structure. He leads the band using a series of codes that signal musical changes that the whole band understands. For example, when he says 'on the one, bass', the whole band stops playing except the bass player on the first beat of the next bar. This allows the band to change direction at extremely short notice within the piece, and yet to the casual observer it looks completely rehearsed. Leaders need to be adept at developing and utilising shared symbols, signs and codes.

Compared with most businesses, this is a remarkable achievement. Imagine what would happen if the drummer had to send the guitarist a memo to request a change in tempo or direction within the performance. Imagine also what would happen if they had to hold a focus group to seek approval from the bass player and their family before asking the other members about the set list.

An example of focused chaos

IDEO is widely respected as one of the foremost innovation design consultancies in the world. It has been responsible for product innovations in computer technology, consumer goods and industrial products. Here are some of the important features of the IDEO culture.

Diverse people

Making differences a source of creative advantage. IDEO often puts together a team that comprises both experts and naïve contributors from areas that at first would seem to make no sense. For example, biologists, sociologists, housewives, chefs and so on are brought together to design a microwave oven. By using experts from other disciplines, you can gather information about a product more quickly than through simply having a bunch of engineers working within their own particular techie culture.

MBA + attitude

Backing up creative thinking with hard analysis, being explicit about real constraints in a given project, rather than introducing them at the end of the creative phase. The use of a systematic process (focused chaos) for problem formulation, data analysis, idea generation, idea improvement, prototyping and concept testing that acts as a flexible template for creativity. The full application of brainstorming principles such as suspending judgement, selecting which ideas to progress and so on. This is far more effective than simply writing a list of ideas on the flipchart and then forgetting them – a process all too common in many businesses.

Permissive leadership

Adopting a leadership style that hires and encourages people who do not always agree with the leader. Arranging a climate that encourages people to customise their personal working environment, in order to have them be playful rather than seek permission to have novel ideas.

What can hinder high performance? We can learn much from music here, particularly the ideas of consonance and dissonance.

Mama Weer All Crazee Now

'We should do something when people say it is crazy. If people say something is good, it means that someone else is already doing it.'

Hajime Mitari, President of Canon

Limits to high performance – Dissonance

Dissonance in music is a mixture of sounds that makes your ears grind with pain or joy. Listen to the beginning guitar phrase to 'Paint It Black' by the Rolling Stones to hear this effect, Jon Lord's keyboard solo on 'Flight of the Rat' from Deep Purple in Rock, the glorious clashing of guitars and viola on 'Venus in Furs' by the Velvet Underground, or 64 minutes of unstructured white noise and feedback on Lou Reed's Metal Machine Music to understand the magnificence of dissonance when used to advantage.

However, dissonance in business can be costly, due to wasted effort, in-adequate responses to problems and internal combustion where meeting time is consumed without any useful outcomes (heat without light). Business guru Jerry Johnson offered us a valuable insight about dissonance in his classic work on this topic. The diagram, taken from top to bottom, shows that businesses have a range of responses to disruptive external changes, including ignorance, consonance and dissonance. Internal politics can kick in, or simply denial. In all cases this leads to an inadequate response to external opportunities or threats with the consequence that the business fails to capitalise on external change. This may account for why Kodak did not see the Polaroid camera on the horizon, and why they failed to predict the impact of digital photography on sales of photographic paper.

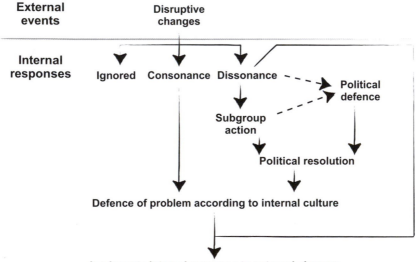

Given that dissonance causes discomfort in business and this turns people off, how can you learn from music how to welcome dissonance as an asset that you can then capitalise on?

Anarchy in the company

Too many bureaucrats spoil your company's ability to deliver new things.

Hire more freedom fighters if you want more innovation.

Deliver us from dissonance

Dissonance in business is all about getting people to work together who wouldn't live together (but might sleep together). This is a clever trick and involves getting people to genuinely value differences rather than just mouthing the words at a corporate team event. So we need consonance of outcome while tolerating or encouraging dissonance of the means of getting there. This is easy to write but harder to do. The norm is to have teams of agreeable people who are largely the same. A couple of examples illustrate the value of consonance and the cost of dissonance.

The value of consonance

Rover consistently outperformed rivals by maintaining consistency of leadership and purpose through the 1990s. They stuck to a few simple principles for a considerable period to drive their business forward, such as: properly implementing a suggestions scheme, which accepted 20 per cent of all suggestions, rewarded idea theft across functions, implemented total-quality principles fully and consistently (further details in *Best Practice Creativity*, page 208). Rover also avoided fad management, where the business is driven by the latest fashions without considering the context. Of course, this golden age eventually came to an end and Rover are no longer trading as I write this. This does not detract from their earlier successes in achieving consonance of purpose and execution. In a sense, Rover transformed from orchestral management to Rock'n'Roll leadership, using both structure and creativity to drive sustainable performance improvement.

The ultimate cost of dissonance

An eighty-year-old man wanted to create a driveway in his garden. He had been given permission by the local authority to do this and commenced work. This involved lowering the pavement and removing a wall. Halfway through the work, the authority asked him to stop. Apparently, he needed two lots of permission – one from the pavement department and the other from the wall department. Although the people in the pavement department sat only metres away from the wall department people, they seemed unable to resolve the matter, as the elderly gentleman had not abided by the protocols of the authority. The dissonance ended up with the authority withdrawing all permissions rather than trying to resolve the matter. They asked the old man to re-erect the wall at a cost of £1,000 to himself. He died shortly afterwards.

Albert Einstein on dissonance

If A equals success, then the formula is:

$$A = X + Y + Z$$

X is work

Y is play

Z is keep your mouth shut

Rage against the machine

In spite of many attempts at reform, the bureaucratic machine rolls on in the following example, which concerns the wastefulness of red tape.

A primary school had to get some repairs done to its building, requiring the erection of some scaffolding for survey work. The school arranged for the scaffolding to be erected, but were unable to appoint builders, since they were obliged to ask the local authority to do this. The local authority person responsible for obtaining quotes did nothing about this for two months. As a result, the school incurred a penalty of £1,200 for keeping the scaffolding. This money could of course have been better spent on education. When asked if the school could have avoided this delay, it transpired that the local authority effectively held a monopoly over the selection of contractors. In other words, if the school had attempted to hire their own people, the authority would have blocked the decision. It's probable that many other authorities waste money in similar ways due to bureaucratic bottlenecks and corporate irresponsibility. In such circumstances it is important to find out how to do things before you start, and prepare to improvise as you go, rather than assume you must do things using the formal systems, discovering weak spots and being clever as you go. All the qualities that keep John Otway going well past the normal longevity for a rock star!

These small examples serve to demonstrate the price of dissonance and the value of consonance in business. Yet, paradoxically, we need dissonance if we are to learn. As management guru Gareth Morgan points out, 'We need processes in organisations that make the undiscussible discussible.' Madonna hit Morgan's nail on the head here by revealing the dark side of organisational life: 'Losing my virginity was a career move.' We'll move on to discuss learning, unlearning and reinvention next, which do require the destabilising influence of dissonance.

Thinking the unthinkable

'We need processes in organisations that make the
 undiscussible discussible.'

Gareth Morgan

'Losing my virginity was a career move.'

Madonna

Learning and unlearning

Successful bands and businesses learn rapidly and continuously. Good learning includes both what Peter Senge calls *single-loop learning* (how can we improve what we are already doing?) and *double-loop learning* (how can we learn from what happened?).

The Beatles reinvented themselves several times during their career, so have David Bowie, Rover and Madonna. The Beatles preserved the same team members in the change process, whereas the other examples were solo artists with a supporting cast, which changed as they changed. It seems as though Madonna and Bowie preferred to work like virtual companies in outsourcing their key employees as they went.

The wisdom in this is that if you want your business to change you need to change the people. Rover did this consistently during the 1990s, when they adopted Japanese work practices, with the result that they consistently outperformed others. The essential strategies for reinvention are those articulated by business gurus Senge, Argyris and the Academy of Rock gurus Madonna, Bowie and Prince:

■ learning to change rapidly – acquiring new knowledge and skills; and

■ unlearning – dumping, rewiring or improving out of date baggage.

The options for unlearning are:

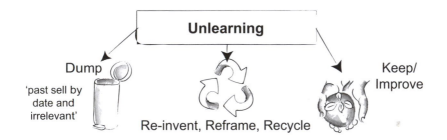

We must review strategies and practices to purge ourselves of stuff that has become out of date. For example, Rover started out making bicycles and then moved into cars. We will see two examples from the rock business that demonstrate learning and unlearning in action. The first is that of the artist called Bill Nelson, who reinvented himself but left some of his audience behind. Our second example took his audience with him, which was ultimately more profitable.

162

The difficulty of unlearning is neatly illustrated by one of the Warner Brothers:

'Who the hell wants to hear actors talk?'

H. M. Warner, Warner Brothers, 1927

And in this story about the Forth Road Bridge:

'It took more than thirty years for the management to realise that tollbooths were not required on both sides of the bridge, since most people who went across the bridge one way needed to come back.'

Scottish Taxi Driver

Reinvention

The tendency in Rock'n'Roll is that, once you have found a successful recipe, you keep repeating it. The band can often make a lot of money out of reproducing the same notes in a slightly different sequence. Their audience often shouts for familiar songs. There is a complex set of collusions that make it hard to forget history. This has worked well for bands throughout the ages. Just look at how Lou Reed has managed most of his career with just two chords configured in different ways, using his expertise with language to tackle different issues and give his songs a unique trademark. Apologies to AC/DC fans in advance (I'm one), but it's a musical truth that most of their repertoire comes from two or three basic chord structures. However, in the rock world, people like Lou Reed and AC/DC are the exception. In most cases, the formula wears out after a year or two and it's all over. Remember Five Star, Dollar, The Nolans? Exactly! In other cases, artists transform themselves, but leave their audience behind, failing to attract a new one.

Dedicated follower of fashion

Unfortunately businesses are also creatures of habit and continue to play their hits long after their audience has left the venue. Sony failed to spot the iPod because they had acquired a music division that had a vested interest in selling music rather than making it accessible via the Internet. Drug companies find it almost impossible to ditch a compound after investing millions, even if it's a complete turkey. We are all creatures of habit. Think about this: the average life of a business is about forty years, with Stora, the Swedish timber products company, the extreme exception at seven hundred years. Management guru Arie de Geus tells us that '40% of all newly created companies last less than ten years' and that 'the average life expectancy of all firms … is only 12.5 years'.

A few artists, such as Madonna and David Bowie, have successfully transformed themselves and taken their audiences with them. These are genuinely interesting, since they have discovered a trick that many people and most businesses have not learned: the secret of longevity through transformation. Can it be discovered, analysed or bottled?

Oops, I did it again ...

The repetitive nature of Rock'n'Roll

Given that there are only twelve notes in an octave, it is a miracle that more musicians and groups do not sound alike! However, as in business, musicians do repeat themselves, sometimes with great success, in other cases with abject failure. Look at some of the most successful repeat performances:

The Beatles – Oasis

Dylan – Springsteen

Queen – The Darkness

Madonna – Britney

A window on personal reinvention

We can learn a great deal from those artists who are sufficiently self-aware to understand their own reinvention dynamics and who are also willing to share their secrets with the world. One such artist is the enigmatic musician/artist known as Bill Nelson. Nelson was the leader of the seventies art school band Be-Bop Deluxe, and performed in a variety of other groups, including collaborations with David Bowie and David Sylvian. More recently he has gained a cult following as an avant-garde musician. Nelson is an artist who has continuously pushed the boundaries of the rock paradigm. As such, he has had immense influence on acts such as The Darkness and Big Country, but his popular appeal has been rather less dramatic.

It is rare for artists to open themselves up to the world of scrutiny. Nelson has risked this in his online diary and in his 2004 book *Diary of a Hyperdreamer*. Over the page are his principles for personal reinvention, originally written as a precursor to producing a new album.

Notice how relevant Bill Nelson's list of principles are to anyone considering their own reinvention or trying to help a business stop repeating its past.

Erasing the past

Radiohead's album *Kid A* is a good example of bold reinvention in an industry that encourages repetition. Faced with an enormous success from their previous album *OK Computer*, they might have been tempted to rewrite this album. Instead they adopted a completely different approach.

There are previous echoes of this bold behaviour in the form of Pink Floyd's follow-up to *Dark Side of the Moon*.

Bill Nelson's principles for reinvention

1. Be afraid of neither the future nor the past but make a mark on the moment.

2. Do not give in to the temptation to elicit favour.

3. Resist the obvious but embrace it when it becomes perverse to do so.

4. When gazing in the mirror, look for the artist rather than the guitarist.

5. Build a bridge between melody and dissonance.

6. Do not be afraid of the 'off' switch.

7. Hang no hopes or importance on your actions.

8. Act only when there are no alternatives to stasis.

9. When no words appear, refuse to sing.

10. Ignore all extraneous noise.

11. Cease to seduce.

12. Trust the muse, she always knows best.

Source: *Dreamsville* – the Bill Nelson Website (www.billnelson.com)

© Martin Bostock

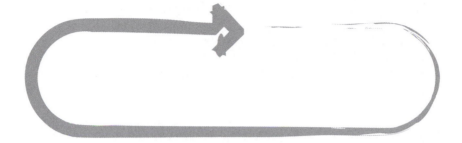

John Maynard Keynes on reinvention, learning and unlearning:

'The difficulty lies, not in the new ideas, but in escaping the old ones …'

Lou Reed on learning:

'Half my mind is taken up with old Rock'n'Roll lyrics rather than what I learned at school.'

Nelson's reinvention principles applied

Bill Nelson's personal wisdom translates well into a business context. In making 'a mark on the moment', we need to find a unique position that can be sustained for longer than our competitors can. However, we have to do better than best if we are talking unique and sustainable for longer than others can manage. As I write, Pfizer face this problem as the world's number-one healthcare company. Where can you go when you are number one? There is always the danger that complacency will set in.

When we are about to do something new, 'trust the muse' means that we focus on intuition rather than rely on existing research. Because we live in a world that is drowning in data, we tend to downplay intuition. Recall the Cornflake Girl story on page 52.

Acting 'only when there are no alternatives to stasis' reminds us to examine all alternatives before making a decision on critical issues. This is not a recipe for not making decisions! Examining alternatives requires us to synthesise options, to bring alternatives together that will produce better options rather than compromises. This requires the use of *and/also* thinking rather than *on/off* thinking.

Many complex decisions are not 'shall I or shan't I?' and it does not pay to treat them in this simplistic way. Under pressure there is a great tendency to make binary *on/off* decisions; it is this tendency that separates professionals from amateurs, sheep from goats, leaders from managers.

Not-only-but-also thinking

Some simple decision making in business uses *either/or* (*on/off*) thinking. This could be thought of as 'digital' in the way that a light switch is either on or off.

Most problems are not so clear-cut, and require an 'on the one hand/on the other hand' approach, and this requires *and/also* thinking. This could be thought of as 'analogue', in the way that a dimmer switch offers a range of lighting options.

Analogue thinking requires a *synthesis* of alternative choices in order to come up with resolution.

Bart Kosko compared digital versus analogue approaches to life in his work on fuzzy thinking. Put simply:

Digital	Analogue
A or not A	A and not A
Exact	Partial
On/off	Continuum
Either/or	And/also

The comic geniuses Peter Cook and Dudley Moore summed this up in the title of their famous TV series, *Not Only But Also*.

The following example shows how analogue decisions can be superior to digital ones.

A company sold a product exclusively to one customer. Wanting to grow, the company decided to sell to other customers in the same market. The exclusive customer threatened to cease trading if this happened. One of the company's senior sales managers offered the customer a price advantage for two years and the transfer of exclusivity to a related product. They accepted this. Three years later, business in the sector had doubled and business with the exclusive customer had grown by 40 per cent. Prior to this analogue decision, the sales manager had been given the digital instruction to 'JFDI' (Just Forget your stupid idea and Do It) by a director. If he had acted 'digitally' they would have lost their loyal customer, and suffered any damage that might have ensued.

171

Nelson's reinvention principles applied

'Refuse to sing when no words appear' would be a good lesson for many businesses to learn. Why do most songs have to have lyrics? Why do most websites have to have text? Why do most businesses have departments they don't need? And so on.

Nelson's 'off' switch is curious. What could it mean in business terms? Is this the ultimate distinction between art and business? Many businesses would be better off if they were to adopt this principle of stopping doing what is no longer wanted or needed rather than carrying on regardless. There is often an irresistible temptation to continue in the face of compelling evidence of the need to do something different. Kodak recently experienced this with the death of conventional film processing. Had they chosen to notice the trend some years back, they might have been in a better position to respond to market changes.

'When gazing in the mirror, look for the artist rather than the guitarist' relates to the business of making good choices. What implicit or explicit criteria do you or your business use to assess temptations? Do you have a clear idea of the difference between the 'artist' (who you are and why you are on Planet Earth) and the 'guitarist' (what you do for a living, to keep yourself occupied, and so on)? Is there a link between *who* and *what?*

Leaders need to constantly refer themselves back to the vital questions, 'What business am I really in? and 'What is this business here for?' They then devise a strategy that connects what is done to the higher purpose, rather than a series of disconnected expedient moves.

In the ever-changing age we live in, it is wise, having established a clear strategy, to build in the capacity to be flexible. A strategy is not a fixed plan, but one that responds to the realities and pace of change of the business cycle. Nelson's 'build a bridge between melody and dissonance' equates to the need to balance stability with new ventures that spoil the balance sheet in the short-term.

Key point

Bill Nelson may be considered to be mostly an inventor in so far as he has refused to consider what some of his audience wants in his reinvention. A consequence of this is that he has succeeded at reinventing himself, but at the cost of losing some of his following. However, his reinvention principles are highly transferable. Look further at Bill Nelson's list and consider the effects of your own reinvention on your relationships. We shall next follow the career of a reinvention master who took his following with him.

Too many cooks ...

Mother was preparing the ham joint. Before she put it in the oven, she cut the end off. Her young daughter asked, 'Mummy, why do you always cut the end off the ham joint?' Mother said, 'I've no idea, darling. Now run along and play.'

Not satisfied, the little girl turned to her grandmother and asked her the same question. Her grandmother smiled and said, 'Well, my dear, in my day we used to have a small oven.'

Reinvention while taking your customers with you

Many rock bands fail (just think back to the point on super group comparison on pages 62-3) and it would be cool to look at the reasons why they do so and the parallels with business failure, but this is for another day. We have already seen how John Otway transformed himself into an almost impossible to copy niche player. We have also seen how Bill Nelson led his own personal reinvention. Now we'll look at another example from a rock star who has embraced mass marketing as well as reinvention. This will give us some clues as to why U2, the Rolling Stones and McCartney are still successful with valuable transferable lessons for business.

Finding a focus

Our candidate began performing music when he was thirteen years old, learning the saxophone while he was at high school and began playing in a number of mod bands. All these bands released singles, which were generally ignored, yet he continued performing. The following year, he released the music-hall-styled 'Laughing Gnome'. Upon completing the record, he spent several weeks in a Buddhist monastery. Having left the monastery he formed a mime company – a non-obvious career move. This was short-lived, and he formed an experimental art group in 1969. This, of course, is David Bowie.

Getting the right raw materials – Bowie as an HR manager

As necessity is the mother of invention, Bowie needed to finance the art group, so he signed a record deal. His first album featured 'Space Oddity', which became a major hit single in the UK. He began miming at T Rex concerts, eventually touring with Marc Bolan's bassist/producer Tony Visconti and guitarist Mick Ronson. The band quickly fell apart, yet Bowie and Ronson continued to work together. The next album, *The Man who Sold the World*, did not gain much attention. Following the release of *Hunky Dory*, featuring Ronson and keyboardist Rick Wakeman, Bowie developed his most famous incarnation, Ziggy Stardust. Bowie quickly followed *The Rise and Fall of Ziggy Stardust and the Spiders of Mars* with *Aladdin Sane*. Not only did he record a new album that year, but he also produced Lou Reed's *Transformer*, the Stooge's *Raw Power* and Mott the Hoople's *All the Young Dudes*, for which he also wrote the title track.

Rock'n'Roll HR

Bowie has always shown an amazing ability to surround himself with talented people. Perhaps this is one of his biggest sources of longevity.

Re-engineering the corporation – Bowie as changemaster

Bowie unexpectedly announced his retirement from live performances during his final show in 1973. He retreated from the spotlight to work on a musical adaptation of George Orwell's *1984*, transforming the work into *Diamond Dogs*. The album was released to generally poor reviews, yet it generated the hit single 'Rebel Rebel'. Bowie supported the album with an American tour. As the tour progressed, Bowie became fascinated with soul music. He subsequently refashioned his group into a Philly soul band and revamped his image in a sophisticated stylish way. The change took fans by surprise. *Young Americans*, released in 1975, was the culmination of Bowie's soul obsession, and it became his first major crossover hit, peaking in the American Top Ten and generating his first US number-one hit in 'Fame', a song he co-wrote with John Lennon and guitarist Carlos Alomar.

Daring to challenge the rock paradigm – Bowie as an artist

Once in Berlin, Bowie began studying art and took up painting. He also developed a fascination with German electronic music, and Brian Eno included his particular brand on their first album together, *Low*. Released early in 1977, *Low* was a startling mixture of electronics, pop and avant-garde technique. It received mixed reviews, yet was a highly influential album in the late seventies, as was its follow-up, *Heroes*.

If you want people to change, change the people – Bowie as process re-engineer

In 1983 Bowie released *Let's Dance*. He recruited Chic guitarist Nile Rodgers to produce the album, giving the record a sleek, funky foundation, and hired the unknown Stevie Ray Vaughan as lead guitarist. *Let's Dance* became his most successful record.

Sledgehammer

'If it ain't broke, we've still got a chance to fix it.'

Mike Hammer, Management Guru

Pablo Picasso possibly commenting in advance on Mike Hammer:

'Every act of creation is first of all an act of
  destruction.'

Pablo Picasso

Chinese wisdom on Sledgehammers:

'The nail that sticks up will be hammered down.'

Anon

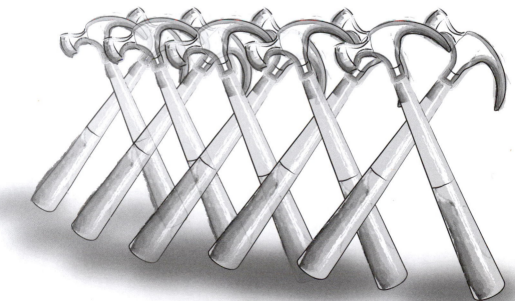

When change is over, change again – Bowie as magician

Bowie's next project was less successful. He formed a guitar rock band called Tin Machine. They released an eponymous album to poor reviews and supported it with a small tour, which was only moderately successful. Tin Machine released a second album, *Tin Machine II*, which was ignored. On this occasion, the magic did not work. Time to change again …

Forming innovative partnerships – Bowie as networker

In 1995 Bowie teamed up once again with Brian Eno to produce *Outside* and went on tour, co-headlining with Nine Inch Nails to lure a younger audience, but his strategy failed. In 1996 he recorded *Earthling*, an album heavily influenced by techno and drum and bass. *Earthling* received positive reviews, yet it did little to attract a new audience. Many techno purists criticised Bowie for exploiting their subculture. It seemed that his attempt to cross demographic and culture divides was not going to work on this occasion. Since then Bowie has formed partnerships with a number of artists, including Placebo, and reinvented himself as a brand for a US online bank.

The main learnings from this dramatic series of reinventions include:

- make radical changes, even when your current strategy is successful;
- hire and work with the best people you can find, especially if they are better than you;
- read the environment and engage with new movements when they are more than fads; and
- learn from failure and quickly move on.

Reinvention unplugged

Bertrand Russell on reinvention:
'Be isolated, be ignored, be attacked,
be in doubt, be frightened, but do not be silenced.'

Andrei Voznesensky on reinvention:
'The art of creation is older than the art of killing.'

'Silence of the Cows'
Abbie Hoffman on reinvention:
'Sacred cows make the best hamburger.'

Summary

High performance requires preparation, delivery/execution and learning/reinvention – not necessarily in this order.

Spend more time on stage than in the studio or at the backstage party at work. Balance rehearsal and review with the ability to profit from improvisation. Sometimes fewer meetings at work make for smoother delivery.

One tried and tested formula for successful delivery comes from John Otway and goes something like this: begin with the end in mind; do the hard work; deal with details as well as the big picture; if what you are doing isn't working, do something different; above all, enjoy what you do.

Unlearning is required for reinvention, yet unlearning is much harder than learning because it requires conscious effort to forget recipes laid down through experience. Bill Nelson reinvented himself but left some of his audience behind. David Bowie reinvented himself several times, taking his audience with him and gaining new followers. How good is your business at unhooking itself from worn-out recipes without losing customers or markets?

A few rock stars have reinvented themselves, taking their followers with them. There are many parallels between their experience and what you must do to renew yourself personally. What lessons can be learned from John Otway, Bill Nelson and David Bowie in this respect?

Questions to ask back at the ranch

More questions to pose next time you're on stage:

1. If your staff are using more energy on the dance floor than on the factory floor, how can you make your factory more enticing/compelling? In other words, how can you make your company a great place to work?

2. How do you get yourself into the zone so that you can turn it on when you really need it?

3. How do you start work as though you had already reached the encore?

Epilogue

Let it Roll

The Applications

The Rock'n'Roll competence framework

You might think that a competence framework is a little bit more orchestral than it is Rock'n'Roll. Hold on a moment. On the one hand you are right. In some cases competence frameworks have become a self-serving justification of the HR profession's salaries and sense of self importance. Lists of competencies are sometimes so long that the poor devils who have to use them neither have the time to read them nor understand the jargon they contain if they do. Worst of all, work does not come in compartments but in bundles of capabilities. As soon as competence frameworks get linked to pay, some people start collecting hundreds of examples to demonstrate they deserve what are usually very small pay increments. In doing so, the real work all but stops. It bloody well makes me so mad, I wanna write a rock song about it!

Rock'n'Roll also has structure; it is not just about making things up as you go along. An absence of structure leads to chaos. So, of course, there has to be a Rock'n'Roll competence framework in this book – 'Isn't it ironic?' as Alanis Morissette would have said. I've noticed through many years of conversations with business leaders that the things that bug them seem to revolve around relationships, motivation, leadership and getting high performance. In other words, Sex, Drugs and Rock'n'Roll. Just think. At a trivial level, having a set of Rock'n'Roll competences might just make performance appraisals more bearable. Imagine if the boss said, 'Well Pat, you've done well on "Rock'n'Roll" this year, but you need to work on "Sex" next year. The options to help you are: self-abuse [distance-learning MBA]; group sex [in-house training course]; and cross-dressing [job rotation]. Which best fits your learning style and aspirations?'

Seriously, I'm proud to offer you the Rock'n'Roll competence framework as a starting point for your own thinking on the subject. There can be no standard recipe for what matters most for high performance, as much of it is industry-specific. However, I have found that this framework gives people a pretty good start, as it helps start the conversation about what matters most in their organisation. This framework is in plain English, is relatively short and offers things that people can actually see, hear and experience rather than vague platitudes. It has three clear levels of achievement: Initiate, Improve and Innovate. If you are going to use a competence approach, this is a good starting point. Treat them as suggestions, provocations, challenges to come up with something better, more specific, better fitted to what you actually do.

Logic and physique

Max Born (fellow scientist): Do you believe that everything can be expressed scientifically?

Albert Einstein: Yes, it would be possible, but it would make no sense. It would be description without meaning – as if you described a Beethoven symphony as a variation of wave pressure.

In the same way, some competence frameworks miss the essence of what makes us special.

Sex

Sex, a.k.a. relationships

Making bonds with suppliers, colleagues, customers and partners that give you the edge

INITIATES – Forms relationships

1. Gains rapport with people of similar and different persuasions.

2. Makes the first move in establishing new work relationships.

3. Identifies and prioritises the wants and needs of others.

4. Demonstrates insight into key stakeholder issues where the business can add value and communicates these benefits in a concise and compelling way.

5. Differentiates between important and key stakeholders using objective criteria when difficult choices must be made regarding priorities or resources.

6. Develops relationships both within and across functional and geographical divides in the business.

7. Builds networks and opens their network up to help the business extend its reach beyond its natural size.

8. Uses language that others understand and adapts communications content for different audiences.

9. Engages others by using the most appropriate media for the message and for the receiver's communication preferences.

10. Identifies and uses nonverbal behaviours to develop work relationships.

Sex, a.k.a. relationships

Making bonds with suppliers, colleagues, customers and partners that give you the edge

IMPROVES – Develops relationships

11. Reinforces the importance of relationships both in words and deeds – in other words, makes others feel good about work.

12. Seeks stakeholder feedback (formal/informal) that can give the business the edge.

13. Uses power (arising from position, resources, expertise, information, networks) in relationships, leading to positive advantages for all concerned.

14. Invests energy in maintaining existing relationships; treats people with respect.

15. Builds persuasive arguments for new business opportunities and/ or resolves problems in a clear and concise manner.

16. Prepares the ground when important decisions are to be taken by setting up opportunities to influence key people.

17. Chooses the right time and place to influence individuals and groups.

18. Works to identify common goals and outcomes rather than focusing on differences between individuals and groups.

19. Facilitates others to help them make difficult decisions.

20. Leads opinion with professional bodies and participates in industry opinion-forming bodies.

Sex, a.k.a. relationships

Making bonds with suppliers, colleagues, customers and partners that give you the edge

INNOVATES – Changes relationships

21. Takes notice of and acts upon the feelings and concerns of others in an interaction.

22. Raises performance or relationship problems openly and in ways that are likely to improve the outcome for both parties in the long-term.

23. Will take a stand against strong personal agendas when business critical issues are at stake.

24. Supports and praises others.

25. Focuses on the problem rather than the person in a difficult encounter.

26. Communicates complex information in ways that others understand.

27. Uses both the formal and informal communication systems to influence key issues.

28. Works collaboratively on projects in order to create win–win outcomes for the business and other parties.

29. Develops positive relationships with key suppliers, colleagues, customers and partners.

30. Puts bad work relationships back on the rails rather than letting them wither or infect others.

Drugs

Drugs, a.k.a. motivation and leadership

Energising ourselves and others to do their very best

INITIATES – Motivates self

1. Sets potent and challenging personal goals.
2. Does whatever it takes to reach agreed goals.
3. Sets high personal standards as an example to others.
4. Can organise work appropriately to meet a range of deadlines.
5. Acts to avoid unnecessary distractions from key objectives.
6. Is resilient in the face of obstacles.
7. Delegates tasks effectively.
8. Shares own leadership strategies to help others understand the rationale for their behaviour.
9. Aligns own behaviour with business values, especially in challenging business conditions.
10. Conveys a sense of belief in self and others through their actions and reactions.

Drugs, a.k.a. motivation and leadership

Energising ourselves and others to do their very best

IMPROVES – Leads others

11. Finds out what makes others tick and uses this information to motivate them.

12. Designs work to enhance other people's personal preferences wherever possible.

13. Challenges others to exceed their expectations.

14. Recognises and makes others aware of their special talents and development needs.

15. Works towards win–win outcomes for individuals and teams whenever possible.

16. Uses participative methods in meetings and within teams to ensure that all contribute.

17. Distributes the benefits of success by publicly praising teams and individuals for a job well done or extraordinary effort irrespective of the outcome.

18. Operates a zero-tolerance approach towards behaviour that undermines the values of the organisation.

19. Treats others fairly and honestly.

20. Explores difficult issues that could block performance.

Drugs, a.k.a. motivation and leadership

Energising ourselves and others to do their very best

INNOVATES – Leads change

21. Uses a range of leadership styles to instigate change (tell, sell, consult, delegate, empower and so on) consistent with the needs of the task, the people, and the situation.

22. Models the behaviours of successful leaders both inside and outside the business and encourages others to do the same.

23. Constantly reviews business habits, removes those that are obsolete, and introduces new practices that can benefit the business.

24. Makes bold decisions, inspires and aligns others with the overall plan.

25. Adopts a variety of different perspectives to understand and resolve conflict.

26. Deals positively with situations that are or could be seen as stressful or threatening.

27. Acts decisively to take urgent action when there is insufficient data or incomplete information.

28. Supports, rewards and recognises others who are curious and creative.

29. Builds own and others' ideas into practical and profitable innovations.

30. Encourages a climate of openness and exploration.

Rock'n'Roll

Rock'n'Roll, a.k.a. performance and delivery

Doing the hard work and improving the way we work on a continuing basis

INITIATES – Gets things done

1. Uses a systematic approach to planning and organisation to ensure tasks and projects are delivered on time and within budget.
2. Prioritises the projects with the highest long-term value to the organisation.
3. Translates strategy into goals that inspire others to do their best.
4. Takes care of both small and large aspects of a task so that implementation proceeds efficiently.
5. Identifies a range of potential options when making decisions.
6. Uses a range of analytical and creative problem-solving techniques and processes to deal with unforeseen situations.
7. Considers ideas at different levels of generality when dealing with complex issues.
8. Evaluates risks and consequences before committing to a course of action.
9. Recommends changes that are clear, positive and compelling.
10. Uses a wide range of sources of information to find opportunities for giving the business the edge.

Rock'n'Roll, a.k.a. performance and delivery

Doing the hard work and improving the way we work on a continuing basis

IMPROVES – Enhances the way things are done

11. Creates meaningful and measurable performance indicators so that everyone knows what is to be delivered and when.

12. Links short-term must-do activities to long-term strategies.

13. Strives to achieve and maintain a right-first-time approach to business.

14. Identifies different and original ways to improve or replace existing processes or systems.

15. Develops others in the business using a variety of methods: advice, coaching, mentoring, structured development, training and so on.

16. Makes decisions that balance risks against projected returns in both the short- and long-term.

17. Constantly challenges the idea of what outstanding performance looks like in practice so that the business may improve over time.

18. Treats mistakes as opportunities for learning and improvement.

19. Spots the need for renewal and change before current strategies and actions are starting to underperform.

20. 'Looks in other places' to find new and better ways of working – using suppliers, colleagues, customers and partners as a valuable source of new product/service ideas.

Rock'n'Roll, a.k.a. performance and delivery

Doing the hard work and improving the way we work on a continuing basis

INNOVATES – Changes the way things are done

21. Finds ways to use time, money and people more effectively and efficiently.

22. Identifies new ways of enhancing existing products and services.

23. Creates potent, desirable and actionable visions rather than daydreams.

24. Introduces unpopular ideas in the face of opposition when there is a compelling case for their introduction.

25. Pursues continuous quality improvement as a way of life.

26. Introduces innovative work practices into the business where these lead to improved performance.

27. Encourages self and others to learn by actively seeking out new ways to do old and new things.

28. Demonstrates energy, drive and passion for innovation.

29. Minimises risks associated with innovation by developing prototypes or models that allow concepts to be tested at low cost.

30. Strikes a balance between actions that maintain short- and medium-term cash generation and speculative long-term profitability.

Now, just for serious fun ...

Here come ...

The Top 20 Rock'n'Roll Leadership Tips

The consultant formerly known as Peter Cook performs in his country'n'western glam-rock duo, The Cowpokers.

This three-piece duo play occasionally as a distraction from work. Some people need to play golf to relax, others play guitar.

The Top 20 Rock'n'Roll tips

1. Good vibrations: How can you get your customers to fully experience what you do, in their hearts as well as in their heads?

2. (If paradise is) half as nice: When introducing people to what you do, how can you signal that the first experience is only the foreplay and there is much more to come?

3. Knowing me, knowing you: If you want to serve someone really well, find out their wants, needs, whims, foibles, fancies, fantasies, fanaticisms and ensure that what you are offering touches the parts that others cannot or dare not reach.

4. Nothing compares 2 U: Make your offer unique and hard to copy.

5. It ain't what you do, it's the way that you do it: If there are no product differentiators, it comes down to the experience: service delivery and responsiveness.

6. Suspicious minds: Adopt a zero-tolerance approach to destructive political games in your business.

7. Don't let me be misunderstood: Get your message clear and make sure those you are communicating with are awake, alert and in receive mode.

8. U got the look: Style always overwhelms substance. Once you have substance sorted, go for style every time.

9. The great pretender: Leadership requires you to be a master of style. Dictator, salesperson, facilitator, confidant, comedian, entertainer, counsellor. Know your own range.

10. Puppet on a string: Don't encourage cult followers. They will never tell you when you are wrong, especially when it matters. On the other hand, do encourage people who will tell you where you are going wrong. That's the way you are going to learn.

11. You ain't seen nothin' yet: Once you have got your clients hooked on your service delivery, find ways to up the game before they get bored with the same old service and have a 'business affair.'

12. This town ain't big enough for the both of us: Competitive strategy is about differentiation rather than trying to fight it out in an overcrowded market. If you must do this, play to win.

13. Video killed the radio star: It's not the competition you know about that kills you. It's the unexpected entrants to a market that wipe out the need for your product overnight. Make sure you look out for unexpected market entrants.

14. I can't control myself: Creativity without discipline rarely leads to innovation.

15. All shook up: Learn to ride the waves of chaos at work rather than running away from the unknown, unstable and unexpected.

16. How can I be sure?: To make great decisions, balance analysis and data with intuition and attitude.

17. I've got you under my skin: Keep your customers faithful by ensuring they embed your business into theirs at a subcutaneous level of integration.

18. I still haven't found what I'm looking for: Strategy is a process of continuous learning and reconnaissance.

19. We gotta get out of this place: If your market is disappearing or your strategy is not working, just doing what you do harder and faster will not help. Press the 'off' button and do something different.

20. Come together: When something good happens at work, make sure you all experience the joy of text simultaneously.

Bubbling under ...

21. Walk on the wild side: Encourage the mavericks, Madonnas, prima donnas, belladonna and anacondas at work.

22. Better the devil you know: Don't be afraid of organisational dissonance. If something sounds funny, it might need more investigation, but don't stop the music.

23. Don't look back in anger: Organisational learning should not be a blame game. A dispassionate review of successes and failures should be done so that the business can profit from learning.

24. Won't get fooled again: If something does go wrong, do something different. The only mistake is not learning from mistakes.

25. Poison: Don't let unhealthy political 'games without frontiers' become the main occupation of your business. Use antidotes and anecdotes to kill poisoners. In other words, become a champion game player yourself so that you can out-game the amateurs. Over time, move others towards more healthy games.

Now, for takeaway value ...

Here come ...

The Top 10 Questions to provoke your business into action

Cor baby, that's really me! The author rocks with punk icon and two-hit wonder John Otway in a corporate conference at the Brands Hatch racing circuit.

The Top 10 Questions

1. It's the end of the world as we know it (and I feel fine)? How can you create comfort with the unknown and unknowable, so that people are willing bring their soul to work?

2. Shake, rattle and roll? How much creativity and improvisation can you handle? In what circumstances do you need to apply structure and scores to the workplace?

3. What's new pussycat? How do you involve your present and potential audiences in defining new and unknown product/service needs?

4. I'm too sexy? What turns your customers on about what you do? Why do some of them want it all the time and why do others lose their appetite?

5. Simply the best? If you gave your business strategy a song title and/or a short chorus, what would it be?

6. Love is the drug? Where can you get natural highs at work legally?

7. I feel fine? Why do your people come (to work)? Ask what would make them come more often.

8. Changes? Highly successful rock stars manage to change the relationship between themselves and their audiences without losing their following. Successful leaders also manage to change assumptions, values and beliefs over time, taking people with them. How can you take others with you and maintain good relationships?

9. Complete control? Who is generating the sheet music in your company? Can you give them something less damaging to do (or get them a job with one of your competitors)?

10. Speed king? How many speeds does your company work at? Can it do 16, 33$^1/_3$, 45 and 78 r.p.m.? Who is your company's drummer? How do you motivate them?

Now, for further interest ...

Here comes ...

Recommended viewing, reading, doing, listening

Much hullabaloo about nothing …

'Genital Sparrow rock the Scouts' Jamboree'

Spoof hard-rock band Genital Sparrow performing at a participative jam session we organised for 2000 scouts. You might think that scouting is not Rock'n'Roll. Think again! We were surprised at how much these people rocked, performing songs from Hendrix, Nirvana, Bowie, Madonna, Electric Six, Spinal Tap, the Blues Brothers and Metallica.

Recommended Viewing, Reading, Doing, Listening

Here is a list of recommended videos/DVDs, books, things to do and music to listen to. Unfortunately, there isn't space to capture everything that should be here. Because music is a very personal taste, I've confined myself to a few selections that are signposts in some of the directions where you can go to alter your thinking.

 **Watch It**

Stiff Upper Lip – AC/DC Live (2001)

It's not clever and classical but it is Rock'n'Roll, and you will like it. AC/DC come on stage as if they had already reached the encore. High-voltage stuff!

School of Rock (2003)

An extremely entertaining film with an underlying deeper message about accelerated learning.

This is Spinal Tap, Spinal Tap (1984)

The classic rockumentary film with transferable messages in it for anyone interested in the business of chaos.

It's a Wonderful Life (1946)

In my opinion MBA graduates should watch this classic film about a man who gets to see the effects his actions and attitude have made on other people's lives. Such is his impact that they alter their business decisions accordingly.

Masters from the Vaults, Deep Purple (2003)

Watch a bunch of people who could not get on together performing magic spells. Masters of improvisation within a structure, there are moments of true genius here.

The Day The Earth Stood Still (1951)

Classic sci-fi film. Makes you think.

Read It

Weird Ideas That Work **– Robert I Sutton, Allen Lane, London (2002)**

A challenge to conventional thinking about how innovation works.

***Cor Baby, That's Really ME!*, John Otway, Cherry Red Books, London (1998)**

A case study in energy, entrepreneurship and emotional resilience. Also entertaining!

***21 Leaders for the 21st Century*, Fons Trompenaars and Charles Hampden Turner, Capstone Publishing Ltd, Oxford (2001)**

A lofty but worthy tome. Rock'n'Roll it is not, but it may persuade you to see leadership differently.

***Diary of a Hyperdreamer*, Bill Nelson, Pomona Press, Hebden Bridge (2004)**

A rare insight into the life of an artist who moves from the profane to the mundane and back again.

***The Art of War for Executives*, Donald G Krause, Nicholas Brealey Publishing, London (1996)**

An up-to-date rework of Sun Tzu's principles for leaders.

***Images of Organization*, Gareth Morgan, Sage Publications (USA), Thousand Oaks, CA (1986)**

Brilliant on metaphor and its application to complexity.

***Diary of a Rock'n'Roll Star*, Ian Hunter, Independent Music Press, Church Stretton (1996)**

Life on the road. The real Sex, Drugs and Rock'n'Roll manual.

***Insights of Genius*, Arthur I Miller, Springer-Verlag, New York (1996)**

A brilliant compendium of imagery and creativity in science and art.

Tragically I was an Only Twin, Peter Cook, Arrow, London (2003)

Not related …

Best Practice Creativity, Peter Cook, Gower Publishing Ltd, Aldershot (1998)

My first book, which focuses on the art and practice of creativity and innovation at work.

Karaoke Capitalism, Jonas Ridderstråle and Kjell Nordström, FT Prentice Hall, Harlow (2004)

Two Swedish professors bring macro- and microeconomics into intimate contact with Eminem.

The Timewaster Letters, Robin Cooper, Michael O'Mara Books Ltd, London (2004)

Great fun!

Creativity and Innovation for Managers, Brian Clegg, Butterworth-Heinemann, London (1999)

Brian is a physicist. I started life as a chemist. As we know, physicists are from Venus and chemists from Mars. But, strangely, Brian and I have a great rapport in the way we look at subjects such as creativity and innovation. Brian has authored a wide range of titles and has a great resource at www.cul.co.uk.

Strange, Richard Strange, André Deutsch, London (2002)

The dark side of Rock'n'Roll. Richard Strange fronted the seventies cult underground group the Doctors of Madness. This book is not for the faint-hearted or squeamish.

Training with a Beat, Lenn Millbower, Stylus Publishing, Sterling, VA (2000)

Master of accelerated learning using music, Lenn is somewhere on the same asteroid belt as I am regarding our outlook on work, learning and play.

Good to Great, Jim Collins, Random House Business Books, London (2001)

Not rock, but worth reading to rock your leadership paradigm!

Jamming: The Art and Discipline of Business Creativity, John Kao, HarperCollins Business, London (1997)

This is the other end of the Rock'n'Roll spectrum – uses jazz as an organisation metaphor. John offers us some management 'riffs'.

Leadership Ensemble, Harvey Seifter and Peter Economy, Times Books, New York (2001)

Again, this is the other pole of Rock'n'Roll where the conductor leads the band.

Lost in Music, Giles Smith, Picador, London (2000).

An account of the ridiculous business that is Rock'n'Roll.

 **Do It**

Attend a jam session either to participate or watch from a safe distance. You will learn about structure, improvisation, band politics, communication and conflict all in one evening!

Go to some concerts outside your field of interest – rock, blues, jazz, salsa, soul, funk etc. You must experience this – its not good enough watching it on TV.

Start a rap about music and leadership at work. Surprise yourself at what others know about the topic and open up some entirely new ways to see old things.

Join our web forum. Contribute to and gain from an online jam session there. Email us for more details.

Give a talk on the music of leadership. We have a range of general resources to help you do this. Contact us on ++ 44 (0)1634 855267 / 573788 or by email at webmaster@humandynamics.demon.co.uk or on the web www.humandynamics.demon.co.uk.

Organise a leadership jam session or a conference where you can learn about leadership through a variety of different media. Again, we can help with this in terms of design, delivery or aftercare, or all three.

Swap your music with others, but insist that they lend you stuff you don't really like and vice versa. If pan pipes do not do it for you, try getting a new pair of ears for the day. If Beethoven rocks your world, try Bolan. If the Stereophonics are your passion, try Stravinsky.

Listen To It

Like a Prayer, Madonna (1989)

Forget the sensationalism of the title track and listen without prejudice. Some of these pieces touch your heart. Try 'Promise to Try' or 'Oh Father' if you have previously written Madge off as a pop tart. Her work on the *Evita* soundtrack will also challenge your notions of who Madonna is.

New York, Lou Reed (1989)

Reed is a master of language – if he wrote company memos you would read them. His subject matter is real and compelling. If you want to take the hard road, try *Metal Machine Music*, 64 minutes of unstructured feedback. You will either love it or hate it, but you will not be able to deny that this is one place where 'art' has beaten the desires of record company executives to put music out that will sell records. Highly recommended is 'Songs For Drella' by Reed and John Cale, which tells the story of Andy Warhol and the Factory, which was essentially a business incubator for musicians and artists.

The Sensual World, Kate Bush (1989)

How much talent can you get in one person? No need for a duo with Kate Bush. She writes it all, performs it, produces it. A rare talent.

Purple Rain, Prince (1990)

A classic. 'Nuff said. 'Darling Nikki', 'I Would Die 4 U' and 'Beautiful Ones' also essential. The film is worth a look as well, if you can stand the purple one's dress sense. Opinions vary …

Anything by Django Reinhardt

Just because it's clever. How come a man who lost two fingers in a fire can play better than most of us with a full set? Gypsy jazz is not for everyone, so be warned. You might begin to understand John Kao's material on jazz and genius from this.

The Romance of Sustain, Bill Nelson (2003)

A specialist interest possibly, but this album contains some truly beautiful pieces. The track 'For Stuart' was written specially by Bill to commemorate the death of Stuart Adamson, guitarist of Big Country, who admired Bill's wonderful guitar work. The piece evokes both triumph and lament and is true testimony to the power of music as the language of emotional literacy.

Listen Without Prejudice, George Michael (1990)

Just do what it says on the label!

The Shutov Assembly, Brian Eno (1992)

Hard to choose just one thing from Eno, but I had to. Fairly dark, but provocative. 'Plateaux of Mirror' with Harold Budd is excellent for introspection and thinking.

Leftism, Leftfield (1995)

A manifesto for cool introspection and creativity. Lots more good stuff out there, just not enough space to list it all.

'The Cheeky Song' – The Cheeky Girls (2002)

Love them or hate them, the Cheeky Girls illustrate perfectly the fact that good pop music gets into your head instantly and changes your life in three minutes. This is a bit of a tall order in the case of the Cheeky Girls, who have no social message like Bob Dylan. Sometimes this is just nice! Guaranteed, you won't be able to get the chorus line out of your head. Tacky but simply great. Same principle applies to all classic pop music – Abba, Duran Duran, S Club, Robbie Williams, whether you like it or not. I wanna rock DJ …

I also challenge you to listen to some modern artists. Some people I know who like music stopped liking it at the age of 27 and snobbishly claim that new bands are just not the same as the ones they liked in the seventies. Try Avril Lavigne, Moby, Beyoncé, Usher, Busted, Razorlight and more. Add your own items in. Keep on keepin' on …

References and Credits

Prologue

The Creative Priority: Driving Innovative Business in the Real World, Jerry Hirshberg, HarperCollins Business, London (1999).

Jamming: The Art and Discipline of Business Creativity, John Kao, HarperCollins Business, London (1997).

Leadership Ensemble, Harvey Seifter and Peter Economy, Times Books, New York (2001).

Sex

'I'm Your Man', as performed by Wham. Words by George Michael. © Morrison Leahy Music Ltd. Lyrics reproduced by kind permission of the publisher.

Materials on Oticon can be found in *Karaoke Capitalism*, Jonas Ridderstråle and Kjell Nordström, FT Prentice Hall, Harlow (2004). Find them online at www.oticon.com.

Materials on the team cycle developed from original materials by Bruce W Tuckman, *Measuring Educational Outcomes*, Harcourt Brace Jovanovitch, New York (1975).

Materials on The Beatles and Teamwork kindly supplied by John MacCarfrae, Director, Maverick Training, who focus on providing exciting training solutions.

Cultures and Organizations: *Software of the Mind*. Geert Hofstede, McGraw-Hill, New York (1991).

'Orgasm Addict', written by Howard Devoto and Pete Shelley. Published by Mute Song Ltd and Complete Music. Performed by the Buzzcocks.

Drugs

Materials on motivation developed from original materials by Maslow, Herzberg and Vroom, written up in *Working in Organizations*, Andrew Kakabadse, Ron Ludlow and Susan Vinnicombe, Penguin Business, London (2005).

Uncertainty matrix developed from an idea kindly supplied by Alan Drummond of Argenta Europ Limited. Alan's thoughts are built on discussions with a number of colleagues working in this field. See www.argenta-europ.com.

Rock'n'Roll

Materials on Göran Ekvall taken from 'A fertile grounding', by Jane Pickard, originally published in *People Management*, 24 October 1996, and reproduced with permission.

Materials on Pfizer from a public forum on organisational development at Pfizer.

IDEO material kindly supplied by Deborah Richardson on behalf of IDEO. For further information on IDEO see their website, www.ideo.com.

Materials on complexity, systems thinking and chaos inspired by *Strategic Management and Organisational Dynamics: The Challenge of Complexity*, Ralph D. Stacey, FT Prentice Hall, Harlow (2002); and *The Fifth Discipline: The Art and Practice of the Learning Organization*, Peter M. Senge, Transworld, London (1990).

John Otway's website can be found at www.johnotway.com. Human Dynamics also arrange corporate conferences and events with John, combining substantial educational/business content with pure enjoyment/entertainment. Serious fun: a powerful mixture!

Materials on Jerry Johnson adapted from *Readings in Strategic Management*, David Asch and Cliff Bowman, Palgrave Macmillan, London (1989).

Bill Nelson's principles for reinvention taken from Bill's personal web diary at www.billnelson.com. Also available in *Diary of a Hyperdreamer*, Bill Nelson, Pomona Press, Hebden Bridge (2004).

Materials on fuzzy thinking adapted from *Fuzzy Thinking*, Bart Kosko, Hyperion Books, New York (1993).

Statistics about the longevity of companies from *The Living Company*, Arie de Geus, Nicholas Brealey Publishing, London (1997), pp. 8–9.

Photographs kindly provided by Steve Crispe and Peter Birkett. Steve is a professional photographer and expert guitar player (www.stevecrispe.com). Peter runs Das Ist Design, a bespoke graphics design consultancy (email: dasistdesign@talk21.com).